RASHMI URDHWARESHE

WOMEN And The WORKPLACE

A Gender Neutral Approach to Carving Successful Careers

Popular Prakashan

www.popularprakashan.com

Published by
Harsha Bhatkal for
Popular Prakashan Pvt. Ltd.
301, Mahalaxmi Chambers
22, Bhulabhai Desai Road
Mumbai 400026
info@popularprakashan.com

First Published 2022

(4537)
ISBN 978-81-955127-4-4

Cover image: Alamy
Design: Anjali Sawant
Layout: Thinq Mediia

Printed In India
by Manipal Technologies Limited
Manipal, Karnataka

Contents

Foreword

I first met Rashmi when I was on the interview panel for the selection of the new Director of ARAI. She did not get any special marks for her gender but was selected as we felt that she had the experience, capability, and drive to steer ARAI through a time when the world and India were going through a major change in automotive regulations. Subsequently, I was elected the Vice President and then the President of the ARAI and we had an excellent working relationship based on mutual trust and respect. Under her leadership, ARAI's performance not only exceeded in achieving business goals but also helped India set a new dimension to the fast-changing emission and safety regulations. Cordial relations and the development of the team members were the hallmarks of her career.

Her sincere, forthright, committed, fair but firm leadership reassured the Governing Council of ARAI about her appointment as Director. I have closely seen how effortlessly she could handle technology challenges on one hand and delicately balance all the stakeholders' divergent interests on the other hand. No wonder industry leaders would share with me their positive feedback about the excellent services and capabilities of the ARAI. Thanks to Rashmi's high business ethics, excellent leadership in E-mobility, vehicular safety, emission regulations, alternative energy and many more, ARAI had transformed itself into a very vibrant R&D house as well as Homologation centre.

Significant resources from the ARAI were channelised towards supporting the Government of India in establishing technically sound Safety and Emission regulations and thus we at ARAI became the epicentre of technology discussions and negotiations, not just at the national but also at the international level. Rashmi, along with her senior team, provided the much-needed strong anchor. The team ensured to always maintain the critical balance between Government policies, Industry progress and the growth of the organisation.

I also observed that along with having a strong hold on strategic leadership, Rashmi had a very keen interest and zeal towards process improvement and business excellence. After all, she is a trained quality professional, in addition to having several other qualifications that she has acquired during career development! Starting her career as a Trainee Engineer, her rise through the ranks to take the coveted position as CEO (Director) in an organisation of international repute is truly inspiring. Her strong and successful career is rightfully recognised with several awards for research, technology, leadership, women Empowerment, etc. The most notable of them being the "Nari Shakti Award 2019" which was conferred on her by the Hon'ble President of India.

Her own struggle, the pursuit of creating a strong and sustaining organisation and teams, research experiences and international exposure have enriched her mind and brought clarity in thought. On top of it, she is an excellent communicator and passionate about motivating young women and men alike.

I am therefore very happy that she has decided to pen down all her wisdom in creating this book.

Manufacturing in general and the Automotive industry in particular, is often considered a male-dominated sector. In fact, diversity and inclusion are core values of modern and forward-looking organisations, yet much is needed to be done to achieve the desired levels of diversity. Men (and women, equally) need to be inclusive and performing as strong teams, and they need guidance at every step. Building up a strong career requires commitment, motivation, and a clear direction. Professional counsellors and self-help books are abundantly available. But I am doubtful if one single book has earlier covered all the aspects of career development in the Indian context, and especially written by a woman author with a gender-neutral pen!

Organisations in modern India need to prepare themselves to nurture individual growth while focussing on the business. A strong framework is therefore needed to be created with consensus at all levels. Employer's perspective is often quite different from that of the employees when it comes to handling the human resource, their aspirations, team dynamics, role assignments and providing the right workplaces to nurture diversity and inclusion. A beautiful confluence of employee-employer perspectives narrated in the book will be a very welcome outcome for the corporates. The book thus has a place on the table of every professional/leader and the bookshelf of every organisation.

Right from the hard facts of life to women empowerment, the book covers it all. Career steps and preparing oneself from time to time to face challenges and take up changing and more demanding roles are clearly brought out. Interesting case studies and anecdotes about stereotyping make the reader experience the situations in person. Gender-specific details are handled in a very sensitive manner, with the right balance and respect for every individual. Working in teams, taking up leadership roles, handling lady bosses and lady subordinates are addressed with wonderful ease.

I am particularly happy to note that very interesting highlights of sector-specific opportunities and challenges are covered in the book, which would be very useful for young professionals. Significant coverage is given to the topic of why and how to maintain a work-life balance. The case studies also bring out simple but creative approaches adopted by specific individuals.

Getting ready for the future is always very challenging, especially with the rapid technological transformations. The book delightfully covers very important trends that are poised to shape the future for the new and practising professionals alike.

Reading the book is very enjoyable due to the simple but precise language. The subject itself has a great appeal to everyone. The book opens up important and intricate details without losing sight of the bigger picture. Appropriate sketches, especially covering the topic under discussion, an excellent mix of research material, case studies, personal narrative, and critical/directional thoughts will have a great appeal at all levels.

True to Rashmi's usual style of working, she has studied several research journals, papers, national/international data, reference materials and has also carried out specific research to arrive at very sound conclusions. Her rich experience of more than 38 years reflects in the authentic treatment of every point that she wants to make.

The title of the book might give the impression that it is exclusively about and for women. Surprisingly, it is more for the men to better understand their women colleagues in a more scientific manner. Most of the topics covered can be directly applicable to anybody who wishes to be more serious about his/her career. Although the author's strength is in the technology domain, she has covered the other sectors with equal ease (such as women in agriculture).

I have no doubt that the book would provide great handholding for individuals as well as corporates in creating better workplaces!

My best wishes for the success of this book.

Vikram Kirloskar
Vice Chairman
Toyota Kirloskar Motor
Bengaluru, India

Chapter 1

Facts of Life

Workplaces and their dynamics are very interesting but complex subjects, and their implications touch our lives to a great deal, either directly or indirectly. Diversity and inclusion are some of the important values that the matured economies would look forward to nurturing. But the extent of diversity needs to be exploited to the fullest. As Steven Covey puts it, "Strength lies in differences, not in similarities." While we strive to achieve this in our lives, some facts would continue to influence our social and professional behaviours. To know these facts would give us a better chance of achieving what we aim to do in our careers.

Gender ratio in India

As per the report of The Technical Group on Population Projections, India's projected population in 2021 is 136.13 crore with 48.04% female population (as against 51.96% male population). The projected average annual exponential growth rate of the population has declined from 1.63 in 2011 to 1.27 in 2016 and is likely to further decline to 1.07 in 2021. During this period, a similar trend is also projected for the female and male populations.

Sex ratio, defined, as the number of females per thousand males, is an important social indicator to measure the extent of prevailing equality between males and females in a society at a given point of time.

A notable increase in the sex ratio has been recorded in Delhi (5.7%), Chandigarh (5.3%) and Arunachal Pradesh (5.0%). It is noteworthy that India is at the 189th position (out of 201 countries/ territories) in terms of the female to male ratio. With about 110 boys born for every 100 girls, India has the world's 5th most skewed sex ratio at birth after China, Azerbaijan, Vietnam, and Armenia.

While Mother Nature is impartial to women, the society around us does not seem to be! The sex ratio in the country has always remained unfavourable to females.

Health statistics

Some significant health statistics that have an impact on the social and economic behaviour of individuals are:

- In 2018, Age Specific Fertility Rate (ASFR) for the females belonging to the age group 25-29 years was the highest at 146.4 while it was 122.9 for the females in the age group of 20-24 years.
- The ASFR for the age-group 20-24 years decreased from 173.8 in 2015 to 122.9 in 2018 whereas it increased for the age group 30-34 years from 77.6 to 94.7 during the same period.
- The Adolescent (15-19 years) Fertility rate declined from 13.0 in 2017 to 12.2 in 2018. In rural areas, it has significantly decreased from 14.9 to 13.5 whereas urban areas have seen a marginal decrease during the same period.
- The percentage of persons that reported as ailing (PPRA) in last 15-days period is 10.0% (Female) and 8.2% (Male) in urban areas, while it is 7.6% (Female) and 6.1% (Male) in rural areas.

Diversity and Inclusion

Modern-day organisations adopt diversity and inclusion (D&I) as a core value. While the intent is quite clear, it is important to understand the deeper meanings of these terms.

Diversity is recognising, respecting, and celebrating each other's differences. A diverse environment is one with a wide range of backgrounds and mindsets, which nurtures an empowered culture of creativity and innovation. Diversity is usually the range of people in a workplace, for example, people with different ages, castes, religions, ethnicities, people with disabilities, and people identifying with a whole range of gender spectrum. It also means valuing those differences.

Inclusion means creating an environment where everyone feels welcome and valued. It is the achievement of a work environment in which all individuals are treated fairly and respectfully, have equal access to opportunities and resources, and contribute fully to its success.

To be clearer, diversity refers to the traits and characteristics that make people unique while inclusion refers to the behaviours and social norms that ensure people feel welcome.

Inclusivity is crucial for diversity efforts to succeed, and creating an inclusive culture will also prove beneficial for employee engagement and productivity.

Devanshi Joshi is a lovely young girl who was born with Down syndrome. Chapter 9 (Women Empowerment) highlights her inspiring story and how diversity and inclusion, in true spirit enabled her to lead a life of dignity.

Workplace

The term workplace is simple to understand, yet it has a vast scope. It is obviously the location where one goes to work every day. It includes places likc factories, offices, extended offices, and even home offices! The term extends to cover all those places where one is required to go for work. For example, for a health worker, a hospital is a workplace; for an educator, a school or university is a workplace, and so are agriculture fields, research laboratories, underground mines, warships, art studios, courtrooms, and many more for several others.

During the latest COVID-19 pandemic, working from home became the new norm for many, and thus, the definition expanded to include homes! A digital workplace is a very new concept. In a digital workplace, collaboration and teamwork are facilitated by technology rather than by a physical location. But the workplace-related requirements and norms would remain similar, if not the same.

"No road can go where I can go! I can, if I think I can!!" is the spirit of modern woman and that means that society has to create space for women at every workplace! Literally and figuratively.

The workplace is not just a place; it is much beyond it! We spend almost 35 to 40% of our daily time at the workplace! That is the maximum time allocation for any single activity in our lives. At work, I remember having talked about it, especially at the ladies' lunch table. We would lament, grump, and sometimes would also joke about it! At one time, I jokingly said, "On weekends when I drive for leisure, my car turns automatically towards the office road!" One friend mentioned that if she stays away from the office for longer than 3-4 days, she develops an O vitamin (O - Office) deficiency!

Choose a job you love, and you will never have to work a day in your life - Confucius

Gender and gender bias

In the context of human beings, we often use the terms 'sex' and 'gender' interchangeably. However, these two words describe two distinct aspects. It is important to note that sex is a biologically given label but gender is culturally variable. Gender is thus more abstract and varies greatly because we often assign different social and cultural roles to males and females. World Health Organisation (WHO) clearly defines gender as: "Gender refers to the socially constructed characteristics of men and women, such as norms, roles, and relationships of and between groups of men and women. It varies from society to society and can be changed."

Gender bias is thus a tendency of unfairly differentiating and treating men and women. Some people demonstrate deliberate, vicious behaviours against the opposite sex. In the majority of the cases however, there is an unconscious gender bias. Unconscious gender bias can be defined as unintentional and automatic mental associations based on gender, which come from traditions, norms, values, culture and experience.

Fig. 1 - "We remain different but are born to stay complementary."
(Image by Peggy and Macro Lachmann- Anke from Pixabay)

Many cultures do respect the differences between the male and female sexes and believe in their equilibrium. Their complementary forces make up all aspects of the phenomenon of life. Ancient Chinese culture defined that as "Yin and Yang". In the context of Hindu mythology, Shiva and Shakti symbolise that.

This book does not intend to cover gender studies, nor to start a gender war! The purpose is to highlight the reality and expand the vision for better diversity and inclusion in our workplaces.

It is equally important to pay attention to the significance of societal behaviours that impact our professional lives. Biologically, men and women are born to be different in many ways, and they will remain so, perhaps generations after generations. As professionals, employers, employees, entrepreneurs or even plainly as citizens, we should be mindful of these differences. More importantly, our efforts should be to overcome gender biases that invariably manifest themselves in our behaviours, upbringing, and culture. But the good news is, this can be changed! The mere fact that gender is culturally variable as explained above, provides a good chance of overcoming these issues with more matured social behaviours.

Social context of gender

The roots of a strongly patriarchal society surface out in many instances, for example, the birth of a child. Most of us have either experienced or witnessed the Indian ethos of rejoicing the birth of a male child and brooding over the birth of a girl child. Thanks to social reformers like Maharshi Karve and Mahatma Phule, who spent their lives for the upliftment of women in the 19th century, Maharashtra offers excellent opportunities for women's education. In fact, it is one of the most important states when it comes to women's education and empowerment! No wonder the first Indian lady Doctor, Anandibai Joshi, came from Maharashtra and paved the path for many women to follow.

And yet, there exist some rural areas in Maharashtra where occasionally a girl child is named 'Nakushi' literarily meaning, 'The one who is unwanted'! This 'unwanted' girl child suffers such blatant discrimination throughout her life's struggle.

The situation in other states and regions of India is no different. From childhood, girls start getting the not-so-subtle signals of bias, comments, or even stern directions from their parents, teachers, and for that matter, everyone around them. Gender discrimination often begins at home. In fact, based on the external environment, children quickly note that boys and girls are different. Their clothes, choice of colours, toys, abilities, and interests are all externally controlled, and the babies internalise these stereotypes.

In developing economies, where millions live below the poverty line, parents prefer boys primarily due to economic reasons. Boys are considered more 'valuable' assets, a potential source of dowry, and inheritors to the house property. In the changing social norms, it is observed that the fathers who take an active role in childcare and domestic responsibilities, create a positive impact on children, and this contributes in a big way to minimise gender biases. Similarly, mothers, who work and take the financial provider's role in the family, are also likely to minimise gender stereotypes for their children. As the children grow, school, teachers, and the other components of society are likely to create biases among them. The parents, who are conscious of these influences, can prevent gender biases from growing out of control.

Education and schooling have a lasting impact on humans. What we learn, comprehend, and absorb in schools stays with us for very long, if not forever. But schools are also fertile grounds where biases are likely to get created. Children are quick to absorb behavioural patterns by observing other children, seniors, teachers, and everyone around them. Teachers are their role models. But formal teacher training seldom includes techniques to avoid biases among students. Some simple guidelines for teachers would be helpful. All that is needed is to make special efforts to inculcate gender equality (and inclusion) as a core value. Teachers can achieve this by:

- Providing more opportunities to girls to take leadership roles. The physiological and maturity growth rate for school-going girls is supposed to be faster than that of the boys.
- Pointing out the under-representation of females in the textbooks/study materials. Books and curriculum settings often do not have inclusivity built into them.

- Having the same level of expectations from girls and boys. While communicating behavioural expectations, it is useful to have a gender-neutral approach. The girls are often warned, "Be gentle. Don't be boisterous like the boys" while to a boy, the teacher says, "Why are you crying like a girl?"
- Providing the same amount of feedback for their behaviours/ performances in academics. Boys are expected to excel in mathematics, science, sports, elocution, and such fields. Girls are expected to focus more on the arts, languages, social studies, etc.

With urbanisation and globalisation, we have witnessed behavioural and social changes favouring women but a lot more still needs to happen. And it won't happen by itself; it needs sustained efforts, not just from social reformers, but from every individual.

Economic impact

Women and their participation in the workforce are two aspects having a great impact on the economy. Womenfolk of every nation remains fertile, untapped resource and with sustained efforts, mainstream contributions from women give immense boost to the national economy. It is for this reason that several schemes are announced and deployed by the government to increase women's participation.

According to the Human Development Report 2020 from the United Nations Development Programme (UNDP), India ranks 131st on the Human Development Index (HDI). With the HDI at 0.645, India is placed in the medium human development category. Some of the other countries in the medium category are Iraq, Bhutan, Ghana, and Cambodia. The same report also highlights the relative Gender Development Index (GDI) and India's GDI is 0.820. What is disheartening for India is that the GDI for women is at 0.573 and that for men it is 0.699, showing a wide gap. Further on the Gender Inequality Index (GII), India ranks 123rd. The labour force participation rate for women in India was reported to be 20.5% while it was 76.1% for men.

The situation is expected to be better as time advances. However, the latest report on Global Gender Gap by the World Economic

Forum says it's the other way round. According to this report, in the year 2021, India has slipped 28 places and the GII gap between men and women has further widened by 3%.

These and many other indicators highlight the need to improve the participation of women in the labour force. Ministry of Women and Child Development, Government of India highlights various schemes that are in force to reduce the disparity between men and women. Improving the socio-economic status of women, increasing their participation in various fields, giving equal rights and opportunities are some of the focus areas.

Fig. 2 - Opportunities for women (Artist- Durga Tilak)

Conventionally it is expected that with the growth in GDP, more jobs would be available for women. Also, with increasing educational and vocational capability development, women's participation is expected to grow in the workforce. But the Indian experience has been the opposite! Despite the growth in GDP, there is a net drop in the participation of women in the workforce for the last 3 years. There are several possible explanations offered by social economists. Some theories that are worth mentioning here are:

- Societal factors govern women's participation in the labour force to a large extent. There is still a widespread belief that when a woman supports the home income, it indicates that the men in the house do not have adequate capabilities to handle the financial load by themselves! Perhaps this holds back the women to step out and engage themselves in economic activities (jobs - either part-time or full time, entrepreneurship, small enterprises, or such).
- A low LFPR (labour force participation ratio) is also seen among educated women. It has been established through

various studies that women with even moderate or high education levels voluntarily drop out from the workforce. Why do they acquire the qualifications in the first place? Perhaps because moderate education increases their potential to get married into higher-income families or elite classes. Such girls are valued by the prospective grooms because moderate education helps the families in managing several economic activities, gives them social status and later helps in the schooling of children.

- Dr. Nileema Limaye, a Professor of Chemistry in a private Engineering College narrated her experiences with girl students. Many of her girl students passed out, found good alliances, joined their husbands on their assignments (typically overseas), and soon forgot that they had the right skills and formal degrees to make a good career for themselves!
- India has been seeing a jobless growth in GDP. In other words, even if there is an increase in GDP, there is no corresponding increase in the number of jobs. This phenomenon impacts women more than men. It also affects the rural population more than the urban population.
- In societies where household incomes are very low, women LFPR is usually higher, especially with very low education levels. Clear examples are agriculture and related sectors. In India, women's LPFR in agriculture is about 75% and, in this sector, they are made to work for low pay or even no pays.

Opportunities and new frontiers

Women in India are fast closing the higher education gap. As per the 2018-19 higher education statistics, women represented 53% at the Undergraduate level, 69% at MPhil degree level and 42% at PhD level. Under the Pradhan Mantri Kaushal Vikas Yojana, young ladies have undertaken several skilling programmes (Short Term Training). According to the recently published NSDC (National Skill Development Council) data, women candidates perform better than men. "Female candidates outperform male candidates across the training lifecycle, with a lower dropout rate, lower ratio of failed to assessed candidates, and higher ratio of placed to trained candidates," concluded the Gender Analysis report 2020.

Fig. 3 - Women in STEM (Science, Technology, Engineering & Mathematics (Artist- Durga Tilak)

With such an impressive capability and potential in young women, the doors are opening for conventional as well as non-conventional career opportunities for them. Among the conventional careers, the top choices include Teaching, Cabin crew and Hospitality, Entertainment industry, Event management, Medicine and healthcare, Law and administration, Fashion and glamour industry, Beauty, Personal care and fitness, Banking, accounting and financial services, Customer care and Communication, etc.

Non-conventional opportunities are also innumerable, ranging from Space research, Web designing, Autorickshaw/taxi driving, Aviation industry, Geology and mining, and many more. Women are crossing more hurdles to make their impact in new fields. Society must get ready to not just let them in, but also welcome them with an open heart.

Crime against women

Women can be victims of general crimes such as robbery, cheating, murder and so on. However, crimes against women are gender-specific crimes.

Many Indian TV channels thrive on crime investigation shows. These shows are immensely popular. A majority of them involve crimes against women. These shows claim to aim at bringing awareness and thereby reducing crimes. The ever-increasing crime rate does not indicate that this stated objective is fulfilled!

Fig. 4 - Crime against women (Artist- Durga Tilak)

The NCRB (National Crime Records Bureau), which functions under the Union Home Ministry, is tasked with collecting and analysing crime data from across the country (36 states and UTs, and 53 Metropolitan cities). The agency has compiled a three-volume report and recorded an average of 87 rape cases every day in 2019 and 4,05,861 cases of crimes against women during the year. There are some revealing and disheartening facts in the report - "Crimes in India-2019", released by the National Crime Records Bureau. The crime rate registered per lakh women population is 62.4 in 2019, up from the 58.8 in 2018. Some very revealing facts highlighted in this report are:

"Majority of these cases under the Indian Penal Code were registered under 'cruelty by husband or his relatives' (30.9%) followed by 'Assault on women with intent to outrage her modesty' (21.8 %), "kidnapping and abduction of women' (17.9 %)".

Not just women, the figures collated by NCRB also indicate an upward trend in cases linked to crimes against children. From 2018, the crimes against children have gone up by 4.5% in 2019. A total of 1.48 lakh cases of crime against children were registered in 2019, of which 46.6% were cases of kidnapping and 35.3% cases were related to sexual offences.

Gender-based violence in the workplaces

Not just in India, women all over the world find themselves quite vulnerable at their workplaces. Many of the instances of sexual abuse, assault or harassment go unreported. More details about this subject are discussed in Chapter 4: Organisational Framework.

It is worth noting here that sexual harassment and assault are considered violations of human rights. However, unlike child abuse and several others, there is no specific international treaty on this subject. The International Labour Organisation (ILO) is therefore considering drafting an instrument/recommendation on this important enabler for gender diversity.

Despite the legal provisions like the Sexual Harassment and Workplace (Prevention, Prohibition and Redressal) Act - POSH 2013 Act, very few cases actually get reported. When the global #MeToo movement recently created a big stir, inspired by its outreach, several women in India came forward to complain against men. Regrettably, it is said that many such women had to face backlash. They were apparently dragged in defamation lawsuits by their higher-ups and their voices throttled.

Further, a vast majority of India's female workforce is engaged in informal sectors. They work as street vendors, domestic workers, agriculture labourers, construction workers, or have home-based activities. For such workers, poverty, stigma, and vulnerability prevent any reporting of sexual assaults or crimes, leave alone their participation in the #MeToo movement!

With the increasing percentage of the women's workforce, there are very good chances of minimising the cases of crimes against women.

Gender differences: What do medical sciences say?

What makes women different than men? In fact, are they different? There are innumerable studies on a variety of fields to establish the truth. Some of these research findings are worth mentioning here. Let us come to terms with the reality!

Physiology

Greek philosopher Aristotle considered women to be inferior to men in many ways. Out of many of his erroneous conclusions about the differences in physiology, the most profound one was that women have fewer teeth than men! For a person of his intellect and rational mind, he could only open his wife's mouth and count the teeth! In fact, he had two wives! This obviously became a laughing stock much later in medieval times. It always takes time to arrive at the truth!

As we know in modern physiology, there are a few differences (not the number of teeth!), which are either direct or indirect results of the Y chromosome. The most obvious differences are physical appearances and others resulting from hormonal influences. But deep inside our bodies, even small physiological differences do amplify to impact the physical, emotional, neurological, and psychological capabilities of men and women. To cite a simple example, a high amount of testosterone is generated in the male body resulting in masculine behaviour, more physical strength and aggression. So the work that requires more physical strength and endurance can be better performed by males than females.

Neurological

There are some differences in the structures of the brains of both genders. I discussed how these differences impact the sex-specific characteristics with my close friend, Dr Sucheta Mudgerikar, a noted neurologist at Apollo Hospital, Ahmedabad.

She said, "There are differences in the brains of men and women, though subtle. In persons, the brain may look identical but functions differently. In olden days, dissections showed a difference in the weight of the brain but anatomically, there was not much difference. They found that the motor areas of the dominant left lobe were better developed in men than in women. This was because men did more physical labour using more muscle power say, for lifting weights, etc."

She further stated, "Their (men's) inferior parietal lobules were larger, making them better at mathematics, better at judging speed and time. In women, it was found that the areas associated with art, music, communication were better developed. In other words, the right side of the brain that deals with these activities was better developed."

In response to my queries about what women are good at, her response was, "Women have more grey matter, meaning more neurons or cells functioning and they have better connectivity between the two sides of the brain. So, women have better intuition, better ability of analysing situations, and can draw conclusions more accurately."

Dr. Sucheta also added, "Their (women) cerebellums are slightly different too and so reactions to situations may be different. Women use their white matter more, meaning the connections between various brain areas, and are better with languages and multitasking. On the other hand, men have better connections within each lobe (of the brain) from front to back and they use grey matter more and hence have better motor skills and perceptions and are better at task-focused jobs.'

Men and women differ in their use of different parts of the brain to encode memories, sense emotions, recognise faces, solve problems, and make decisions. It is also said that the male brain is predominantly hardwired for understanding and creating systems; the female brain is hardwired for empathy!

Medicine

There are sex-specific diseases (that occur only in particular sex) and sex-related diseases (that are more predominant in one sex than the other). Gender medicine studies such differences. It is a fact that traditional medical research is based on the study of male bodies! Under normal circumstances, such clinical research is applied across the population. Only recently, medical research has recognised that symptoms and responses to treatments may be different for men and women!

As Dr Sucheta said, "In those days, bodies dissected were either those of soldiers who died in battles or criminals with death punishment, so mainly men. Now we have functional MRI and electron microscopy and chemical analysis, etc to define the exact differences. Still, these are no gross differences, at least in brains."

Psychological

It is rather funny when Prof Henry Higgins in *My Fair Lady* puts his long list of complaints about women to Col Pickering.

In the famous hilarious song, "Why Can't a Woman Be More Like a Man?", he babbles down simple situations when women just behave unreasonably. It is a different matter that Professor himself is a male chauvinist, extremely egoistic, and headstrong.

Coming to the question, can a woman behave like a man, there could be innumerable responses. I posed a few questions to psychiatrist Dr Swati Joshi to know if men and women have different psychological behaviours under similar situations at work. Dr Swati explained, "Yes, to some extent, women are more emotional due to the role of female hormones. When it comes to traits like communication and micromanaging things however, these behaviours are more dependent on individual personalities and not necessarily on gender. Persons (both men and women) with obsessive traits micromanage every task."

Women are often said to have different responses in stressful situations. Dr Joshi clarified, "Both men and women normally have the same capacity to bear mental stress. It depends on an individual's coping capability, personality traits, attitude towards life and problem-solving ability."

She added, "However, psychological and cultural stressors are more for women worldwide. These stressors are further enhanced in low or middle-income societies, where patriarchy is the main factor. Hormonal fluctuations and variations are also more in women which adds to her stressors. Just to give an example, premenstrual dysphoric stage in women results in dips in moods. These are sometimes causes of distress and reduce women's ability for a short while."

Industrial psychology

It remains to be seen how employers take these facts into account while planning and building their precious resource, the human resource.

I asked Dr Joshi if there are any other psychological aspects that might restrict the growth of women at any level in their careers. Her response was, "I don't think so! The attitude of many females who do not want to take more challenging or long duty hours jobs due to their other responsibilities (like home, family, children etc.), restricts their growth, not any particular psychological aspect. However, due to the nurturing role of a female, she starts feeling guilty if she is not able to give enough time and contribution at home, particularly to her children. This pulls her back from taking responsible/higher roles in her career."

Finally, Dr. Sucheta had a special message and advice for women (and men) at workplaces, "Having said this, many times, men and women do not realise their potential and never have an aptitude test done to direct them in the right direction. This may be used in workplaces to get better results from employees. There should be counselling sessions to find out the environmental (at home and office) and emotional factors hampering performances. Anatomical differences are only subtle but natural abilities differ as per each person's exposure, experiences and resolve to overcome challenging situations. Anatomy cannot be changed but functioning can be! This can happen with training!

The beauty of the human body and mind is that it can be moulded as per circumstances, opportunities, and one can develop artistic/musical capabilities though the brain is the same as others."

Industrial Health and Safety norms have started recognising these differences and taking an approach to health and safety at work with gender considerations. In this sense, the EU-OSHA (European Agency for Safety and Health at Work) pointed out four approaches to gender:

1. **Gender stereotyped** where differences are accepted or exaggerated. For instance, women are viewed as the weak sex, and they are not given field jobs.
2. **Gender-neutral/blind** where equality is promoted by ignoring differences; there can be hidden discrimination if approaches are based on male norms. For example, the rigorous physical fitness tests required for qualifying for Defence Services. These tests were designed with the male norms in the first place! Applying them directly to females would hardly be justified.
3. **Gender sensitivity** based on the incorporation of gender differences, issues and inequalities into strategies and actions.

For example, permitting flexibility of working to women during maternity period.

4. **Gender mainstreaming** which takes the gender and equality dimension into account in the planning, implementation, and evaluation phases of all policies and activities. For example, developing and deploying strong Diversity and Inclusion policy, nurturing the benefits of diversity.

Depending on the maturity and intent of the organisation, one or a mix of the above strategies becomes helpful in addressing gender issues.

Taking gender-related factors into account will help identify both risk and optimisation factors for women and men that should promote gender equality in health because health systems that are "gender blind" will in turn promote better workplaces for men and women!

Motivation

Having established that men and women are different in certain ways, and those differences need to be nurtured by individuals as well as organisations for better results, it also is a fact that gender has an impact on motivation factors.

The subject has been researched and the outcome is quite useful in building up a highly motivated workforce with gender diversity. Some of the key motivating factors are known to be:

- Pay and monetary compensation to a large extent remains one of the big motivators!
- Recognition for good work, praise, responsiveness to requests, growth opportunity, etc.
- Empowerment regarding resource utilisation, overall status and span of control, structure
- Fun, pleasant, enjoyable work environment
- Role and work content, significance/value for the organisation, impact on society
- Job security and future prospects
- Growth opportunity, acquiring and applying knowledge/skills.
- Alignment with personal vision, dreams, beliefs, values
- Flexibility, ability to maintain work-life balance.

Fig. 5 - Staying motivated (Image by Gerd Altmann from Pixabay)

While no conclusive data is being presented here about gender preferences, one can easily see that these and many other factors appear differently in the priority lists of individuals. Besides, at every phase of the career, priority numbering for motivation factors does change considerably.

References:

1. Crime In India 2019: Statistics Volume 1 (National Crime Records Bureau, Ministry of Home Affairs, Government of India
2. Gender Analysis: PMKVY 2016-2021 Short Term Training (National Skill Development Council)
3. World Review 15 May 2020 (Review Report: As India advances, women workforce participation plummets)
4. Global Generation Gap Index (Press Note dated 7 Feb 2020: Ministry of Women and Child Development, Government of India)
5. ACT/EMP: Unconscious Gender Bias in the Workplace (Research Note August 2017: International Labor Organisation)
6. Women and Men in India 2020 (Report of Social Statistics Division, National Statistical Office, Ministry of Statistics and Program Implementation, Government of India)

Chapter 2

Career Building

Developing right skills

The job market and employability are quite dynamic and ever elusively changing. The creation of jobs and employment opportunities is intricately linked with economic growth and its sustainability. Developed economies have very elaborate plans to match the demand and supply in the key sectors. Here is an interesting case study of medical schooling in Switzerland. It is the outcome of interesting discussions I had with my friends, Aruna and Vivekanandham. We were discussing how their son Hari is coping with his medical schooling in Geneva, where they have settled over the last 3 decades.

Structured human resource development

As Aruna and Vivek informed me, 5 Universities in Switzerland (Geneva, Lausanne, Bale, Bern, and Zurich) offer the 6-year medical degree course. After completing their 13 years of schooling, students can be admitted in the first year at the Medical Faculty in one of these universities.

Students coming from government schools do not need to clear any entrance exams and admission is purely based on merit. Non-Swiss and private school students need to undergo an entry/ admission exam. This differs from University to University and the selection criteria are quite tough.

Although medical studies are free, students are required to pay around 1,000 Swiss francs per year as an examination fee. Study assistance schemes/scholarships are available to minimise the burden. Since the government has entire control over medical education, it sets a ceiling on passing marks in the exams and this is done on a dynamic basis. Cut-offs/ceiling marks are decided in view of the social need, total population and the number of doctors already practising and those needed in the future.

As a result, the proportion of students who are unable to complete their studies is around 25% and it changes every year. Most students leave after the 1st or 2nd year. Students have only one extra chance to redo the examination. If unsuccessful, the student should take any para-medical profession, etc. For example, if Geneva University admits 2,400 students in the first year, only 120 will come out as eligible doctors at the end of the 6th year. The remaining students will have to find alternative career opportunities either in para-medical or other areas.

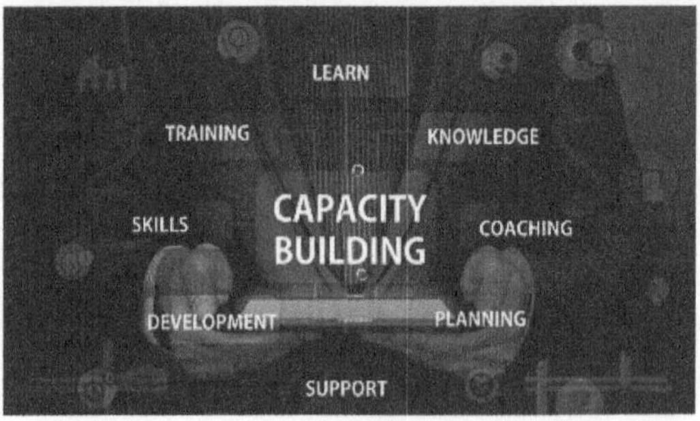

Fig. 1 - Structured human resource development (Illustration from Pixabay)

As indicated in Fig. 1, along with structured human resource development, and close control, these countries also offer social security and other relief measures. The situation in India is quite different and thus it is imperative to track career opportunities and job dynamics during career planning. A formal degree or a diploma from a college may not guarantee a job. However, it places the individual in an advantageous position than others who do not possess such a formal education endorsement. Some of the evident and tangible advantages are listed below:

- A formal degree certainly increases access to the job market which is characteristically quite volatile and demanding.
- Technology, education, and health are three of the most rapidly growing fields and only the most accomplished individuals can do the work. Getting a degree will help one

learn the specific skills and habits needed to make a living in these areas.

- It prepares an individual for specialised jobs. While not all degrees offer a direct route to a job, many are created with a specific career path in mind. An educational degree, for example, is designed as a funnel for teaching jobs; some health degrees also have very specialised jobs waiting for those who complete them.
- Increased marketability is another advantage. In colleges, one gets access to rigorous coursework and prepares one for taking up professional roles.
- It paves the way for advancements in professional skills and specific knowledge one can acquire stepping on the basic degree.
- It provides immense opportunities for personal growth and self-esteem.

With the degree or a diploma in hand, young men and women often take a plunge into career making. During the early stages and in fact, throughout the entire span of the career build-up, there are demands or requirements from the employer or the job creator for upgrading the existing skills or acquiring new ones.

It is quite intriguing that these requirements for higher or different skills are seldom stated. Changing environment, transformations in business, competition, market scenario and several other aspects create such a demand on human resources.

Digital skills are an example in changing times. After the COVID-19 pandemic hit the world, the entire perspective and business scenario have gone for a spin. Hoping that the world will recover in the near future, several new norms are being established in an attempt to recover, at least partially. The education system has undergone a complete transformation. Using digital and network technology, the schools, colleges, and universities, within relatively short time resumed classrooms, at least remotely. A large number of stakeholders quickly adapted to the changing technology. Those, who have not been able to cope with the sudden disruption, will have to take a deep brunt.

"An investment in knowledge always pays the best interest," said Benjamin Franklin. This is not just true for individuals but more so for societies, countries, and civilisations. Those countries which have invested in knowledge over several centuries can reap the benefits for generations.

Making choices

Life often moves at an extremely fast pace. Professionals find themselves in the whirlpools, whirlwinds of situations. Their days start with challenges, drag on and often end in regrets, repentance and frustrations. Very seldom comes a fulfilling day!

Why does this have to happen so often? Can't we have a choice of not spoiling our moment, day, career or for that matter our life itself? Perhaps we have a choice but do not realise it in the zeal of living an action-packed life. Our subconscious mind is always operating with a zapping speed, and we act according to its directions. What is wrong with it? Nothing, in most of the cases. But the subconscious mind will offer a decision based on our previous knowledge, experience, beliefs and so on, as indicated in Fig 2.

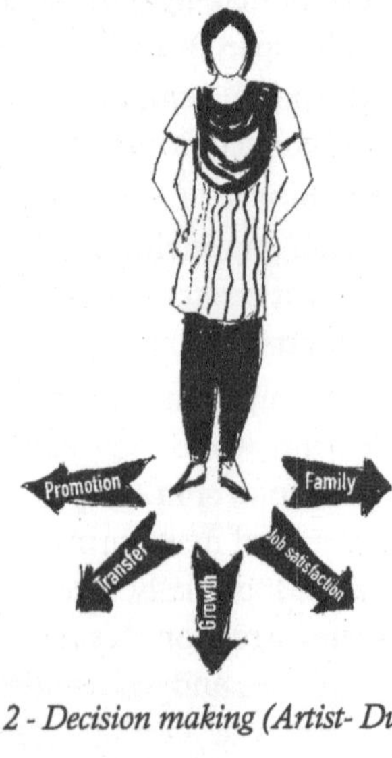

Fig. 2 - Decision making (Artist- Durga Tilak)

Here is an experience, which I came across many years ago. One day, Anagha, my personal assistant approached me with an urgent request to sanction her a half-day leave so that she could immediately proceed home. She was a very committed and efficient secretary and would not normally seek any concessions at work.

I immediately sanctioned her leave but out of concern, asked her if everything was ok. She explained that she expected her in-laws to visit her in the evening, and it being their fasting day, they would need specific food. She had forgotten about it in the morning and hence wanted to go home early so that she could soak Sabudana (sago) early for their fasting meal at night!

I was greatly relieved that there was no major issue but was amazed to know why she wanted to leave early. I offered her some advice. I told her that if she had decided to make Sabudana Khichadi, she could still manage it without going home. She could request the office canteen guy to soak sabudana, and take it with her in the evening. Another option would be to buy ready stuff on the way home. And yet another possible option could be that she could prepare different fasting food which did not require pre-processing! Ultimately, of course, she could take half-day leave and do as per her original plan!

So, that day, Anagha learnt to make choices. These are trivial matters in life, but they teach us to recognise possible options available in certain situations. If we train ourselves to look for options, we are amazed by the results! As they say, we can make better choices if we use both sides of our brain! Every day we are confronted with thousands of decisions, major or minor -- whether to eat chocolate ice cream or not, whether to tell the boss the facts about the project failure or not, whether to ask a friend for a favour or not and many more. How does the brain decide? It is said to rely on two separate networks, one that determines the overall risk versus reward and the second that guides how one ultimately behaves. These cognitive controls and value-based decision making ultimately drive us to make decisions.

Fig. 3 - Cognitive control in decision making
(Image by Mohammad Hassan from Pixabay)

Career choices

Usually, the topmost activity towards the end of formal education is to get the most lucrative job or a dream job. Young men and women in the modern world are quite well informed about the opportunities and options available.

Colleges/universities and finishing schools also offer career guidance centres, which help in identifying and selecting the right jobs. The "Right job" is a rather euphoric situation and young professionals soon find themselves disillusioned. They are not aware that jobs are often created keeping the organisation in mind, not the person! Hence, it is extremely challenging for individuals to fit into them.

The challenge is further enhanced if the job outlines and expectations are not gender-neutral. Women must be mindful of this fact. When selecting a job, it is quite important to keep in view the long-term career goals. One may be required to change the job depending on several circumstances, priorities, choices, etc. However, the overall focus on career development would provide the right direction and enable one to make the right choices.

A special survey was a part of the research work for this book. One aspect of the survey outcome as illustrated in Graph 1 below indicates the most common reasons people change their jobs. The top 5 factors in the order of priority being: better/interesting work content, a better workplace, higher growth opportunities, core values and policies and minimising commuting time.

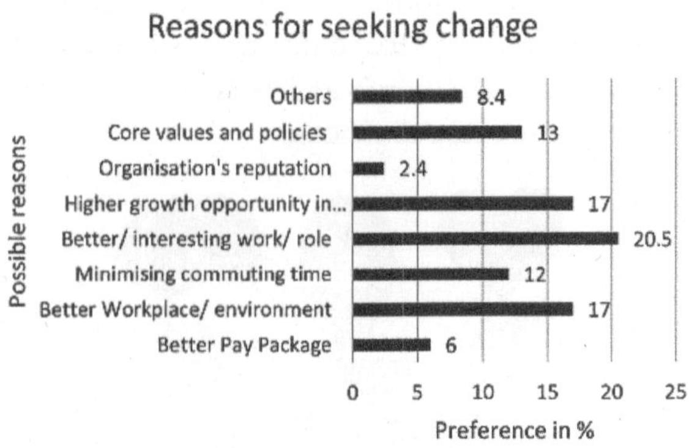

Graph 1 - Survey response: reasons for change of job

Before choosing the right career, one must learn about oneself. Personal values, specific interests, and aptitudes along with the personality type would direct one to the right fit. Several professional tools and techniques are available and should be tried out. Typically, quite simple steps that help in making the right choice are:

- Choosing something you enjoy
- Find a career with a positive outlook and prospects
- Income potential/compensation package
- Career fitting your lifestyle
- Check if there are any barriers to entry

Being able to choose from various options is a great thing and not everyone is fortunate to get that opportunity in the current job situation. With whatever choices exist, one must learn to make the best use of them, especially at the start of one's career.

Aspiring for/accepting a new role

In professional life, an individual comes across many opportunities, better or bigger roles, new challenges and many more. It is often said that opportunity knocks on the door very softly. Women are perceived to be more conservative in their approaches when it comes to accepting these challenges. Why does it happen? It is perhaps because the stability and status quo also offer the much-needed peace of mind for women. Also, some psychological aspects stated in Chapter 1 (Facts of Life) play a role in driving the decisions.

Top performers, irrespective of their gender, are often the prime targets for additional roles because they enjoy challenges and frequently venture out to demonstrate their capabilities. While there is absolutely nothing wrong with accepting additional responsibilities, there is a chance of a quick burn-out. One must be very careful and learn to draw a line so that the plate does not get too full. The guideline for deciding when to push back the additional/new work is:

- When there are chances that your primary job responsibilities will suffer.

- When it is someone else's work. Unless it is strategic and adding value to your work or professional development, it is better to stay away from such instances.
- When there is a no exit strategy and the nature of work is quite vague
- When it would not contribute to your skill sets, growth, or opportunities.

Setting your own boundaries and sticking to them does not show your lack of initiative or ambition. On the other hand, it shows that you prioritise doing the job on hand. The good part of accepting new/additional roles is that it pushes you out of your comfort zone and it is a great opportunity to grow personally and professionally.

One of my friends, working in a government office had shared her experience with me a few years ago. The job being transferrable, all officers, including ladies, were required to accept the transfers. It became really challenging especially due to clashing personal commitments. On top of it, relocating to an unknown place all by oneself was another problem. Everyone's situations were different but they had a similar pattern. Even in the government office, which is otherwise expected to be less flexible, a suitable solution was tried out to tackle the problem. Ladies were transferred in rotation for a year or two at a time, at a particular posting location. It became much convenient for the lady officers to handle the transfers. It so happened over the years that the ladies found a nice way of teaming up. They would share a good apartment house, support each other, and more so, even learn to enjoy their lives despite being away from families! The 2-3 years would thus pass pretty much with ease, and it would be time for going back. The officers, when they came back to their hometown, would certainly have attained great confidence in themselves, be more empowered and more importantly, be ready for taking higher challenges and new roles!

On several other occasions, I have come across many colleagues, not just ladies, who have difficulties in accepting new challenges that involve relocation or a change in role. I remember a long discussion with Ashutosh, a young colleague. He was a bright executive with an excellent flair for technical marketing. We were looking for posting someone in Delhi, who could liaison with the Government Ministries, other R&D Institutes, and cover techno-commercial discussions with customers. My assessment indicated that Ashutosh would be the right choice. It was clearly a great enhancement of his existing role and would open a new horizon for him. It so happened that he assigned higher priorities to his personal commitments and thus declined my offer with a heavy heart!

Learning to be professional

When in a profession, whether in big organisations, small, or even as individual entrepreneurs, one is expected to be a "professional". What do we really understand by the term "being professional"? In simple words, it is the etiquette at work, with which one deals with colleagues, bosses, guests, suppliers, and for that matter, with everyone connected around one's profession.

Just the way Aesop tales, Panchatantra Neetikatha and all other wisdom that we learn and absorb during childhood helps build up our personalities, finishing courses also teach us formally how to develop professional behaviour. Not everyone is fortunate to have a formal course but truly speaking, there are some simple tricks that really make the difference and help in adopting better professional behaviour at work. Many organisations have ethical policies, but good behaviours are always taken for granted! Like they say, common sense is not at all common, professionals do not necessarily demonstrate professional behaviour! Some simple tips might be useful:

- Know your organisation, its mission, vision, and overall business and if available, learn its rules and regulations. It helps in establishing a bigger picture for the mind and also helps in aligning your role.
- Regardless of the level, hierarchy, roles, etc. respect others, not just for the work they do but also as human beings. Remember what wonders it did when Munnabhai (in the film *Munnabhai MBBS*) embraced the cleaning staff member, just to appreciate all the good work the grumpy guy was doing to keep the floor clean every day!
- Giving personal space to others is also quite important. Imagine how annoying it is when the colleague sitting next

to you is peeping into your computer screen, overhearing your tele conversations or picking up the extra pencil from your table!

- We Indians tend to be argumentative, just about any subject. We vociferously put forth individual views and hardly have the patience to listen to others.
- Especially in a cross-culture environment, it becomes important to listen to others, wait for your turn and then express concisely! During my visits to countries like Japan, I keenly witnessed these etiquettes. It is considered extremely impolite to interrupt while the other person is talking. Observing others and modulating our behaviour helps to a great extent.
- With it also comes the ability of clear communication, verbal, written or even non-verbal i.e. body language. Good communication skills are assets for professionals. For some, they are inherent, for many others, they have to be acquired. Verbal communication has one more dimension in modern workplaces -- telephones, virtual meetings, and other digital communications. It needs great efforts to be an effective communicator in all available media.
- As a next step, it is also important to manage emotions and use the right language at work. Especially in stressful situations, this ability is of immense value. The use of offensive language is neither professional nor a sign of good personal attributes. One must also learn the ability to tolerate differences. Differences in views, working styles, expressions and so much more!
- In personal, and more so in professional life, time commitment as well as punctuality is a great habit. Having respect for other's time comes as a corollary.

  We are quite familiar with the long waits at the clinics despite going with a proper appointment. I always wonder, how the medical practitioners do not value the patient's time as much as they value their own!
- It takes time and effort to build trust and accountability for each other. It grows with honesty, camaraderie and openness of mind. Another major contributing factor to build trust at the workplace is to maintain confidentiality (with respect to

official/personal information), not engaging in loose talks or petty gossips.

- Trust can further be enhanced by supporting each other and sharing skills and knowledge. As the saying goes, "If you have knowledge, let others light their candle in it"!
- Indulgence (rather over-indulgence!) in social media is becoming a curse in maintaining the right decorum at work. Many organisations have clear policies to cover these behaviours but in the absence of formal directives, an individual's discipline must prevail.
- Staying focused on work, integrity to the work and maintaining positivity not only helps individuals but also spreads goodness all across! Believe me, it is contagious!

Professional behaviour is the key to success and must therefore be nurtured. Most of the behavioural assessments/annual appraisals of individuals invariably include the above in some form or the other.

Career growth trajectories

Each one of us in professional careers gets about 35-36 years of active roles. A career is the sum of jobs onc holds and the accomplishments one achieves in professional life. Some people stay in one industry/workplace or profession for their entire career span, whereas some make one or more changes. If you measure the success in the career by the titles or designations, the growth curve often looks like a 45-degree line, starting from your entry level to the highest post that you are holding or likely to get. It is easy to calibrate one's performance on such a scale.

Fig. 4 - Career growth (Illustration from Pixabay)

Depending on the individual circumstances, capabilities, opportunities, etc., there certainly would be variations in the slope, continuity, and shape of an individual's growth trajectories.

On the other hand, if you assign value to your accomplishments rather than the positions you hold, the nature of the curve is quite different! It is often considered to be a bell curve. It indicates that in the initial years of the career, the pace of acquiring new skills and accomplishments is quite steep. This is the "learning phase of the career". During this phase, one can experiment around, acquire basic skills, and even learn about oneself! Exploring about self, the environment and careers enables young professionals to carve a niche for themselves. It is normally in this phase that job-hopping is quite prevalent. For some, this phase is quite prolonged but it is at the cost of other matured phases to come in the career. After all, everyone has about 35 to 37 years of active career life under normal circumstances. As the popular saying goes, "There are three ingredients of good life - learning, earning and yearning."

For many a noble soul, learning is a lifelong activity but in the context of a career built up, the learning capability tapers down after a certain age/maturity. The learning curve, therefore, flattens midway and starts declining.

The latter half of the curve thus largely controls how the previously acquired accomplishments are used or applied during the course of the second phase of the career. Mastering the niche or building on the strengths and consolidating the activities enable to bring a strong career focus.

Earning or monetising what one has acquired can be quite enriching and rewarding. For some professionals, it could be large paycheques; for some, it could be excellent innovations and technologies, and for some others, it could be their enhanced image as domain experts and other rewards and recognitions.

What is the motivation for a professional to transcend his Earning phase to reach the Yearning phase? Quite intriguing but that is where one starts yearning or having a deep desire and longing for something. In most successful careers, the longing towards the end of the earning phase is the deep desire to do something for others. Giving back to the organisation, to colleagues or even society is a strong motivator. It thus comes as no surprise that many a great leader towards the last phase of their professional careers spend substantial resources for the benefit of others. Many great names like Ratan Tata, Azim Premji and such can quickly be recalled, thanks to their social outlook and personal commitments. The resources need not be just monetary; they often involve giving personal time to others, mentoring young colleagues, and documenting the knowledge and wisdom. All these are very significant contributions of the last phase of the career and help in creating/leaving a strong legacy.

In retrospect, when I look at my own career, I can distinctly see these phases standing out! In fact, towards the Yearning phase, I decided to do something that would enable young professionals to build strong careers, and this book is the result of that!

Career planning

At any point, one can start plotting one's own career trajectory. It should normally start where one would like to see oneself at the end of the career! To put it in other words, as Steven Covey's habit 2 says, begin with the end in mind! From there, you can backtrack by identifying what skills are essential at what level. Plan to acquire those skills, look for the opportunities and step up to achieve your career targets. It is not as simple as it sounds in words! But with consistent efforts, one can learn to be more objective and realistic than being a victim either of self-pity or over-confidence.

For women, and for that matter for men also, there are phases in life where the growth slows down, one is required to step back at various occasions and assign due priorities to personal, social or any other commitments governed by one's values and situations.

There is an interesting report in the *International Journal of Social Science & Interdisciplinary Research* (ISSN 2277 3630 IJSSIR, Vol. 2 (6), JUNE (2013). It is available at *www.indianresearchjournals.com.* According to it, the technological revolution aided by liberalisation, privatisation and globalisation has redefined the way people in modern India work. In the last two decades, career trajectories of the Indian workforce have undergone interesting transformations because of better and greater job opportunities that the technology boom created. The IT industry opened the door to unparalleled career opportunities for aspiring young Indians as a result of some inherent advantages of the Indian work environment like the availability of a large talent pool of educated English-speaking but inexpensive labour force, the Indian Government's policy incentives for profit-making IT firms and the natural comparative advantage of the 12-hour time gap with the American continent (where the activities of a vast majority of multinational IT companies are centred), etc. In addition to contributing significantly to the export earnings for the country and creating a handful of new-age entrepreneurs, the IT sector also offered a multitude of employment opportunities to the educated unemployed youth in India, including many attractive options for women. Women welcomed the opportunities offered to them and as a result, a considerable workforce of India's IT-BPO sector is comprising women.

However, research shows that a significant percentage of women employees in the IT sector leave every year. This attrition at the workplace is typically before the age of 30. Consequently, a huge talent pool of women with about 3 to 10 years of work experience, who have taken such career breaks, is created. Hence, though the proportion of women workforce at the entry-level as well as the middle-level management has increased considerably over the years, there is inadequate representation of women at the senior level in the IT sector.

The IT industry is just an illustrative case. Similar trends are observed in other sectors also. There are several ways to handle these situations, some of which are explained below.

Building a career after a break

Although much more common in women, many male professionals too come across situations in their lives that necessitate breaks in their careers. These breaks often arise on account of personal commitments, job situations, health reasons, relocation plans, severe boredom at work, and many more. In the case of women, the most common being marriage, re-location, childbirth, and caregiving to elders. The break can take the form of a sabbatical, which can be paid or unpaid. Sabbaticals were originally only offered to academics and clerics but are now being increasingly offered by companies and utilised by many individuals to rejuvenate themselves.

Breaks, whether planned or unplanned, forced or volunteered, undoubtedly result in rather uncertain and unstable situations. The individual must overcome loads of difficulties and challenges to get back on track after such a break.

Maternity breaks

As stated earlier, out of the most common 4 reasons for women to take a break in their career, childbirth/maternity break needs special attention. Once I was discussing the career hurdles for women with Dr. Vaijayanti Subhedar, a close friend and a renowned practising physician. She had very insightful thoughts to share on how childbirth impacts women physiologically, psychologically as well as socially.

In response to my question about how much gap a woman should plan in her career for childbirth, here was her response. "Nature has endowed motherhood to females in all living beings. Respecting this truth, a woman should give time for an obstetrical career! Ideally, between the age of 22 and 32 years. Ideally, two children, 2 years apart till the younger grows up to 5 years, provided everything goes normally. This does not take into consideration unfortunate situations like abortions, infertility, abnormal child, genetic malfunctions, and such. Obstetric career cannot be shifted beyond biological limits and hence a woman should be ready for breaks or even a late start in her professional career. You know, some Scandinavian countries have very welcome policies giving part time job opportunities for women and even exceedingly long leaves (with or without pay) to cover her absence from job. They often find that women, when they join after years of break, give back much more to their careers!" Further, she added, "Parents also have a great responsibility of giving their best possible genetic combination to the next generation. This can be best achieved during the narrow fertility period of 22 to 30 years of age. Any delayed conception comes with a higher risk of genetic mutations and other risks for the babies."

Maternity, or for that matter paternity, breaks are likely to be much longer but rewarding in many ways. More and more professionals must therefore account for maternity/paternity breaks to address personal and professional priorities. Organisations should also consider this as a very natural phase in the employees' careers.

Challenges of restarting after the break

Recruiters are likely to have an inconsiderate view on the candidates wanting to join after the break. It may sound harsh but especially in the Indian context, job continuity always enhances employability. If you happen to have a break in your career, the job market forces push you back in the line as compared to other candidates.

In such situations, the individual, after repeated failed efforts to seek the job, is likely to get into a trap of desperation. The desperation may lead to accepting lesser pay, lesser role, or even lesser designation. Lesser with respect to her previous role or lesser as compared to others in the organisation. This is a tough challenge to overcome.

In professional settings, it is many times experienced that, personal priorities and challenges are not appreciated. However justified the break may be for the individual, many organisations may not have the right sensitivity. In such cases, the inability to explain the gap is a part of harsh reality.

Long breaks, especially on account of maternity or health reasons, often have an impact on personal agility, zeal, energy and even time allocation. To do quick bootstrapping and stay motivated to take a new start is challenging, especially for women.

There are chances that during the long absence from an active career, several changes in the work environment would take place. It is necessary to be mindful of the changes in work content, in people, in technologies and then cope with them as one gets ready for the 2nd or any new innings.

Planning a break

Detailed planning of the break often helps overcome the above challenges of getting back on track and catching up with the career. Before considering a break from the career, it is a good idea to plan the gap carefully. Often unplanned breaks lead to people, especially women, never resuming work. This is the greatest pitfall. It needs very strong motivation, physical tenacity, and other support systems to rejoin after the break. Therefore, it helps to find answers to questions like,

Do I need to quit working at this point?

Do I have any other options (such as to work part-time or online)?

What is my deadline for resuming work?

Honestly answering these questions helps in planning exactly how the break is going to be and how one can get back to working afterwards. Planning your break is an essential part of a career gap, without which it gets quite tough resuming work. By clearly reminding the direction of a planned break, there are good chances of return.

Staying connected

During the break, it is essential to stay connected with one's own field, expertise, and key persons. With social media, networking, and the digital world around, this is relatively simple to achieve in today's context than it was 2-3 decades ago. In fact, resuming work requires one to network as much as possible, with people from one's own field and also from outside.

Staying in touch with former colleagues and co-workers to the extent possible also helps in keeping up-to-date with the latest situations and updates of one's interest.

There are some specialised network services/online portals available for helping women to connect with organisations and start their careers after their maternity or other breaks.

Getting ready after the break

Getting a job after a career break could be tough. One must get ready to explain the reasons for taking the break honestly but briefly to the recruiter. Companies often look for professional experience during the career gap. As such, having small freelance practice, informal/formal assignments or projects adds immensely to the resume, sets you in the right direction and even boosts the chances of getting hired by organisations. Even if such assignments may not be paid, the learning and experience gained becomes particularly useful and comes very handy.

The importance of skills while returning to work after a career break should never be undermined. It is essential to keep oneself updated with the new competencies, techniques, or skills in the concerned industry, especially after a long break. Depending on how long the career gap is, the action plan for upgrading the skills should be taken up. A whole lot of self-help options are available through short courses, networking, webinars, and seminars, reading materials, and training programmes to get ready for the plunge.

Sneha holds an MBBS degree with a diploma in clinical research. She had her first baby after about 10 years of marriage. After the maternity break, she was confused about her responsibilities and was not prepared to join back her job. She was helped by some online support groups who suggested 'the earlier the better' and she followed the advice. She joined back the research division of CRF (Chest Research Foundation of CIPLA). Starting with the post of clinical research assistant, she climbed to Head - Drug Division. During her tenure, she brought many revenue-generating projects as well as awards to the institute. In fact, she was the recipient of the best paper award presented in Austria by the John Hopkins Institute.

During all this, she was also helping her husband, Saurabh in the administration of his own business. As his business was expanding faster, she decided to leave the job and join him as a 49% partner. Despite her new role, she is still in touch with her core profession. Recently, during the COVID-19 pandemic, she designed and conducted one certificate course for doctors with an examination at Kolkata.

Gender and career trajectories/paths

It is often debated whether there is any significant difference between the career slope/trajectory of men and women. It is quite clear that taking career breaks or early exits is more commonly observed in women than men. However, those women who are able to overcome the challenges of restarting after the break, are found to be putting in their best efforts to regain their lost time and opportunities. Initially, there could be a lower rate of career progress. However, with sustained efforts and commitment, many successful women have demonstrated their strong abilities and resilience.

There appears to be no statistical data to prove that women professionals have a slower career trajectory than their male counterparts, given that equal opportunities are made available to them. In order to study the relative trajectories, I thought of plotting my own career trajectory alongside my husband's. My husband, Hemant, is also an engineering professional, and we have an age difference of about 3+ years. The comparative trajectories will be quite interesting for the readers!

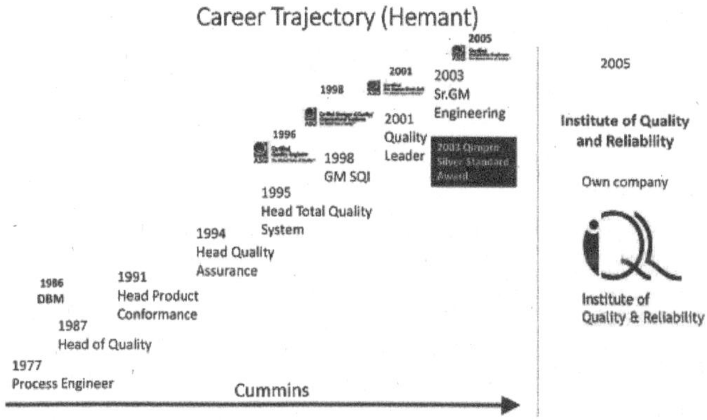

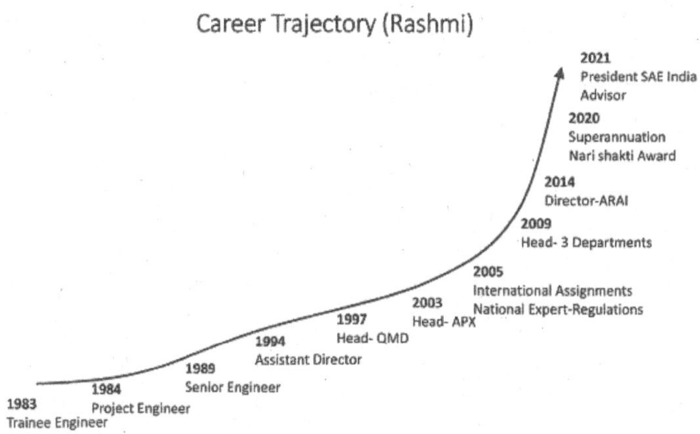

Graph 2 - Growth trajectories

Important decisions in career

Gauri had a PhD (Doctorate degree) in Political Science, and she was a college professor in Dewas having a good start of her career. Then came her marriage and she shifted to Pune. During the transition, she accepted a smaller job, as a secondary school teacher in the campus school, where her husband was a medical officer. As time went by, she found the job simpler, more manageable, and still motivating. Although she was overqualified for the role, she still gave her fullest and is now happy with her choice.

It is quite amusing how the subject of one's expertise may not remain the subject of one's work. Sujata is a pediatrician and took up a job in Maharashtra (Mumbai and Pune) for quite a few years. Her husband, Jagadish, is an entrepreneur and owned a big company. His work involved frequent travels to the USA and at one point in time, he chose to shift the family and settle in the USA. The decision had a long-term impact on Sujata's career. She could no longer pursue her medical profession due to the state laws. After a spell of frustration, she decided to focus on her hobby, classical vocal music. She became a trained musician and took up an alternative and a very divergent career. Some such compelling reasons lead many professionals to take alternative paths.

Changing careers and pivoting

Many people hit a plateau in their careers and feel an urge to change gears or do things differently. In other words, they hit a pivot point in their careers. It allows a person to purposefully change the direction. The earlier generations may have remained loyal to one organisation, just like me. I started and ended my active career in a single place. There are several such persons around us and it's fine to be that way. But that prescription is fast changing now. Gen Y is keen to experiment and take risks at different phases of their careers. Whatever may be the case, it takes time, resources and hustling to pivot from one job description to another.

The most important decision is to identify the right moment for articulating such a change or pivoting the career. This is not just about feeling angry, uncomfortable, or frustrated. One should be clear in mind as to why and how the change will be better for one.

Getting ready for pivoting

After all, when you pivot, there could be spells of unemployment or pay cuts or you could start at a much lower level than the previous engagement. Setting up financial goals and contingency funds helps in creating stability amid such turbulent changes.

The next step would be starting to list down what skills and qualifications you have and more importantly, what skills would be needed in the new role. Honest and truthful self-analysis always helps at this step. Then the next one is obviously to develop and execute the plan to acquire those specific skills in the stipulated time. While still being in the existing role, this step might pose challenges in terms of priority, time allocation, resources, etc.

Once armed with the necessary credentials, it is time to start networking and looking for opportunities in the right direction. It always helps if you build genuine relationships with people who can help you in achieving your objectives.

One can prepare for weeks, months or even years but a career pivot will always carry some risks. Still, it may be worth it because that is often where the greatest opportunities lie!

Let me share the story of my husband Hemant, whose career graph is illustrated earlier. A mechanical engineer by profession, he had a long and successful career at Cummins India Ltd., the erstwhile Kirloskar Cummins Ltd., a multinational engine manufacturing giant located in Pune. In the total span of 28 years at Cummins India, Hemant emerged as an expert in Process Engineering, Quality Management and Reliability Engineering. Still happy with his job, Hemant started with a big dream of making his own mark as a domain expert, consulting professional and trainer in Reliability Engineering and Quality. He had identified that especially in the Indian context, there is a large gap in the skills of professionals in the areas of Reliability, Product Quality and a scientific approach in problem solving. Hemant, therefore, created his mission to contribute to bridging these gaps.

He pivoted his strengths by acquiring independent professional qualifications, namely ASQ (American Society for Quality) Certifications that would establish him as an expert. He was in fact the first in India to acquire some of these certificates like Six Sigma

Black Belt, Master Black Belt, Certified Quality Manager, and such. Having planned his pivot point, he quit his well-established job in the year 2005 and the very next day, incorporated "Institute of Quality and Reliability (IQR)." With a clear direction, resource planning and new personal skills, Hemant successfully achieved his goals. In the last 15 years, under his leadership, IQR has trained more than 5,000 engineering professionals in niche areas. IQR has also helped a spectrum of clients (Defence organisations, automotive giants, other corporates, educational institutes and many more) in quality improvement, business excellence, data analytics, reliability, and other engineering aspects of a business. His career trajectory, which is presented earlier highlights his success story.

Follow your dreams

Fig. 5 - Follow your dreams (Image from Pixabay)

We often listen to motivational speeches and successful people making statements like "Follow your passion" or "choose a job you love, and you'll never work a day in your life" and such. These pieces of advice are passed down for years and they sound incredibly good. The truth is that when wildly successful people give this advice, it represents an idealised image. It does not mean that passion or dreams are not good in shaping up careers. Surely, one should follow dreams but not blindly! Passions fade and change with time, maturity and situations. Passion or dream should thus be used to create a personal mission, which can then be chased.

A mission is much more realistic and directional. In fact, a mission can be a culmination of many more dreams and passions.

Who will forget the strong message of the movie *3 Idiots*! Parents wanting to push their own aspirations on the young children, who are miserable in their studies. It's only when the boys start following their dreams that they achieve something in life.

With a Master's degree and a Doctorate in Chemical Engineering from the USA, Garima Bhatia made an impactful career in the automotive domain. She was a very bright student all through and had passed out with flying colours from IIT Mumbai. Her expertise was diesel exhaust after-treatment material development and technology innovation towards clean air. She has some patents on the subject to her credit. After about 20 years of career, first in the USA and then in India, she decided to quit her job. She then went on to follow her dreams and created a mission for herself. After a very enjoyable phase of handling various projects like birding expeditions worldwide, documenting environment conservation initiatives, arousing interest in young children for nature and many more, Garima is now a well-established nature photographer and birding expert. She has written beautiful illustrative books about birds of specific regions and these books provide excellent guidelines for birding enthusiasts.

References :

1. Career trajectories for men and women professionals in the industry: An empirical study (International Journal of Social Science and Interdisciplinary Research) ISSN 2277 3630 IJSSIR, Vol. 2 (6), JUNE (2013) Online available at *indianresearchjournals.com*)
2. Northeast University: 10 Benefits of having a college degree
3. Digital Magazine 2019 (Developing right skills: a hidden game-changer to tackle today's challenges and build a bright future)

Chapter 3

Workplace Issues

Workplaces are full of challenges! The magnitude and occurrence of these challenges will vary from place to place, time to time and even person to person. In fact, the same work environment can pose quite different problems to different persons. Preparing oneself for handling such challenges would be important for experiencing harmony and enjoying the work. Some typical situations are explained in this chapter.

Workplace bullying

Workplace aggression is a common behavioural situation. Such situations are counterproductive and need to be immediately addressed. In fact, bullying in the workplace is much more common than we think. During the course of the career, most people experience it at some time and, in some form or other. However, for various reasons, such instances often do not get reported in the form of formal complaints.

The term workplace bullying is quite self-explanatory. In simple words, it is a consistent offensive pattern of behaviour from colleagues, subordinates, boss, etc., aimed at a person. Such behaviours can cause serious emotional and mental harm, and in extreme situations, even physical harm. Bullying includes psychological abuse, verbal and non-verbal abuse, and in some cases, even physical abuse. It aims at subjecting the victim to great humiliation and mental agony. At school, university levels, bullying can be often quickly detected, if not eliminated. Unlike schools and colleges, workplace bullying is often subtle. It is quite difficult to address because the offenders still operate within the service rules, norms, and policies of the workplace. Also, workplace bullying happens at a deeper psychological level as compared to bullying in schools and colleges, where it tends to be more physical.

Fig. 1 - Workplace bullying (Artist- Durga Tilak)

Various human and psychological aspects involved in such behaviours are outside the purview of this discussion. But when it comes to disruption of workplace harmony, it becomes an important action point to control. Control is required at both individual and organisational levels.

Bullies are often people at the workplaces who are authoritative, manipulative and hold strong positions in organisations. In some cases, they create some nuisance value around them. Workplace bullying, if left unaddressed, gets only escalated and eventually creates heavy losses to individuals and organisations. There are times when one experiences extreme pressure of some kind in handling work or an assignment. It is often created by someone who has the authority and access to information. The person wishes to show it off to his or her benefit and thus becomes a workplace bully.

Coping with bullying

We are thrown into very vulnerable situations where the opposite party starts bullying by virtue of his authority, seniority, or superiority (whether real, assumed or fictitious!). It is essential for the victim to recognise the motives and intentions to create a protection cover. A vulnerable person can come out of most of these defensive situations through strong willpower, organisational support, and professional handling of the situation.

The key to effectively address workplace bullying and eliminate it from the root is to report the bullying instances quickly and efficiently. This sends a clear message within the organisation that bullying in the workplace will not be tolerated. Unfortunately, many employees are reluctant to report their complaints/experiences because they are not sure what to do, how to speak up and how will the bosses take it. Organisations that strive to reduce the impact of bullying should establish clear and concise disciplinary procedures and follow them when such an incident occurs.

To report workplace bullying to a supervisor or Human Resources Department with facts and details takes a lot of courage and confidence. If despite reporting, things are not resolved or continue to escalate, it may be time to consider looking for employment or a job elsewhere!

It is unrealistic to try to endure workplace bullying. Even the most resilient employees are impacted adversely by continued bullying. Instead, one should focus on making employment decisions that will benefit one's emotional and physical health and prioritise taking care of oneself.

Although the discussion is aimed at how an individual should protect himself/herself against workplace bullying, it equally applies to those who tend to be the ones bullying others! There are instances where individuals who had suffered some kind of abuse themselves, turned into bullies for others!

I came across an interesting study conducted in the year 2008. It states that when women are bullying at the workplace, in more than 80% of the cases, the target is another woman!

Personal experience

Once I was summoned by the office of the Revenue Intelligence. It so happened that they were investigating a case involving an import duty violation by one of the Indian manufacturers. I, being the authority, who granted Homologation certification (Approval in compliance to Central Motor Vehicles Rules - CMVR) for all vehicle models, they were seeking clarification and interpretation of the regulations related to imported vehicles from me. In this incident, I was ordered to bring all homologation-related documents that were related to the manufacturer and also be present in person. The documentation happened to be 30-odd box files, which I took in a sealed suitcase. I was accompanied by another senior officer and a junior officer, who were conversant with the case. We travelled early in the morning from Pune for attending the hearing at 9.30 am in Mumbai.

On arrival, we were informed that the junior officer would not be permitted and during the meeting, we would not have access to our mobile phones. No assistance was made available to us for taking the big suitcase to the fifth floor, where the meeting room was situated!

It was not unusual for me to visit government offices and interact with senior-most bureaucrats. But this incident turned out to be the most gruelling and horrifying experience.

The cross-examination and questioning were handled by quite a senior level, in fact, DG level officer. He and his Assistant Officer asked me the procedures that we followed for granting a Homologation and Type Approval certificate for any vehicle model. It was quite a professional matter, and I elaborated all the details, presented documentary evidence, and concluded the regulatory summary from my side. I further explained that our role was related to testing and verifying compliance with the Motor Vehicle Act and any misrepresentation of facts by the manufacturer for import laws would be obviously outside our purview.

The officers appeared to be disappointed. Perhaps they were unable to get a conclusive statement from my side, which would support their case as per their expectations. They were hoping to conclude that the accused company had violated Indian regulations.

Then they called for a short break, ordered tea (only for themselves), and ignored us for the next 30 minutes or so. On resuming the deliberations, the officer changed his stance completely and started questioning our authority for granting approval for imported vehicles. He kept on repeating his accusation that we had made a grave mistake in approving a model, which did not fit into the import definition. He also asked me to produce the legal document which permitted my organisation to grant approval for imported vehicles.

Surprised at the tone and his words, I had to swallow my anger as well as esteem. I frantically looked in the rule book, fumbled and pleaded again and again that our approval was related to the Motor Vehicle Act compliance and not at all related to import regulation. This drama continued for the next hour or so, till such a time that I was mentally exhausted and emotionally drained.

He then ordered his stenotypist that my statement should be typewritten. He then started dictating the draft. After a few preliminary statements, he decided to announce the lunch break, and three of them started preparing to eat their tiffins. Surprisingly, the officers did not have the basic courtesy to offer help in ordering some food for us, who were respected senior government officers of their levels or even higher!

In a very dejected mood, my senior colleague and I walked out. We were speechless but soon gathered our courage, grabbed something to eat. We discussed at length why the officer in-charge would have treated us the way he did. I soon realised that it was a type of 3rd-degree interrogation for a senior technical officer like me, just to break my confidence and take down my statement under pressure. Why should I yield to his pressure when I had not done any violation myself? What would then be the best way out for us? Perhaps we could ask for more time and come back with legal advice? Submit the written statement once we get back to the office? Or continue to argue based on our technical expertise?

We allowed ourselves time to regain our confidence and after the lunch break, walked in with composure and grace. The officer continued the session. He started dictating the draft of my statement and then I stopped him. I said that if it was being written as my statement, it would be me who would give dictation and not him! He was speechless but understood from my body language that he was dealing with a stronger person. And then in the next hour, we finished the work with the required professional ease and to my own satisfaction. I finished dictating my statement, signed it and we walked off with our position intact!

That day, I came home with a whole lot of strength and confidence in me, but those 6 hours are still etched in my memory as the worst professional ordeal!

Crisis management and female leadership

"There cannot be a stressful crisis next week! My schedule is already full," Henry Kissinger, Former Secretary of State of the USA, said in his characteristic style once! Don't we see it often in our daily routines? Why do such situations arise? How do we handle crisis situations?

What do we understand by the word crisis? A sudden and unexpected event leading to a major unrest/disruption amongst the individuals and the workplace is called an organisation crisis. In other words, a crisis is defined as any emergency that disturbs employees and leads to instability in the organisation. A crisis affects an individual, group, organisation, or society.

Characteristics of crisis

A crisis is a sequence of sudden disturbing events harming the organisation.

The crisis generally arises at short notice.

Crisis triggers a feeling of fear and threat amongst individuals

Fig. 2 - Crisis situation (Artist- Durga Tilak)

Crisis can arise in an organisation due to one or more of the following typical situations:

Technological failure and breakdown of machines, critical controls lead to crisis. Problems in the internet, data corruption, access failures, etc. all result in a crisis in modern times.

A crisis arises when employees have strong disagreements that result in boycotts, strikes for indefinite periods, disputes, and so on.

Violence, thefts, and terrorism at the workplace result in organisation crises.

Neglecting minor issues in the beginning, can lead to a major crisis and a situation of uncertainty at the workplace. The management must have complete control over its employees and should not adopt a casual attitude at work.

Illegal behaviours such as accepting bribes, frauds, data or information tampering all lead to organisation crises.

A crisis arises when organisations fail to settle the dues to creditors and others.

The crisis also arises on account of natural disasters, accidents and similar incidents, situations, or events.

Many of the organisations establish a mechanism to address risk assessment and develop mitigation plans. However, a crisis is quite different from a risk. A crisis is often the result of unforeseen circumstances. Risk is a potential activity or event that could harm the organisation. Thus, to protect the organisation or its people in a crisis often requires different leadership skills and qualities.

Women and crisis management

A Lehigh University and Queens University Belfast research concluded that in certain organisational crisis situations, female leaders have an advantage and edge over male leaders. The study found that the trust established by female leaders practising strong interpersonal skills results in better crisis resolution. They describe this "female leadership trust advantage" in their paper and state that when a crisis hits an organisation, people trust leaders who behave in a rational way, especially so when the leaders are women and when there is a predictable path out of the crisis.

Researchers defined crisis as a common, though often unexpected, time-sensitive, high-impact event that may disrupt organisational functioning and pose relational threats.

Case study

Blue-collar workers can sometimes create crises in organisations for their negotiation benefit. My lady boss and I were once involved in resolving a case of sexual harassment of a junior lady by a senior officer. It was much before the POSH requirements became mandatory for organisations. It so happened that the officer was a rough and tough guy, who headed the Admin and Personnel Department. Most workers found him disagreeable and were looking for any possible behavioural lapses to pin him down. On one occasion, they found it! They got hold of a verbal statement by the lady about the misbehaviour of the officer and converted it into a written complaint against him. The statement was quite vague, completely lacked details and evidence but the subject was sensitive, so it needed immediate attention.

The Director of the Institute was relatively new in his position and when this happened, he was in the Board Meeting. The workers gathered outside the boardroom shouting slogans against the officer. The Director was compelled to come out and give them a hearing. Having sensed the gravity, he summoned a group of executives to seek their advice on handling the crisis. My lady boss and I were a part of that group. After the preliminary discussions, I suggested that the Director immediately announce the appointment of an independent committee to investigate the matter and submit the report on the next working day. That day being Friday and Monday being a closed holiday, it would give us 4 days to complete the investigation and demonstrate a sense of urgency and sensitivity to the employees. Further, the Internal Committee would work under the chairmanship of a woman executive (this was much before the provisions of POSH 2013 came into existence). He immediately accepted the suggestion and as anticipated, the announcement did help in defusing the situation.

We, as committee members, completed our task with full commitment and sensitivity and the investigation report was placed on the Director's desk on Tuesday morning. Women leadership had enabled the committee to develop trust and interpersonal relationships, establish the facts very clearly and arrive at a definitive conclusion and recommendation for the top management. The crisis thus created by a large section of employees was handled by the leadership team quite firmly and sensitively.

Conflict management

Conflicts at the workplace are common and need to be taken in our own stride. Conflicts often arise due to differences in opinions, values, priorities, viewpoints, approaches and sometimes, previous biases. Conflicts result in personal frictions and if not handled in time and in a professional manner, may lead to disruptive situations. There are well-established management techniques and strategies which teach how to handle conflicts.

While it is good and very desirable to take steps to minimise the risk of a conflict, one would not be able to avoid conflict entirely. Therefore, one should acquire the skill to defuse a conflict and make it more productive, when it does arise. Conflict avoidance is not a very constructive strategy at the workplace. Energy should not be wasted on ruminating over a potential conflict that may occur. Difficult interpersonal situations should also not be ignored because they will not disappear just by ignoring them.

The first step to resolve a conflict is to be able to view it objectively and depersonalise it. Looking at the whole issue from above and outside enables the person to overlook the trivial details and focus more on the core. Ancient wisdom also teaches us that conflicts can be resolved using a 4-pronged approach namely, Saam-Daam-Dand-Bhed (Persuade, Purchase, Punish, Exploit the weakness)!

In modern management tools, there is no place for Daam and Bhed but the other two tactics often work when used appropriately! Here are some important techniques of conflict management:

Problem solving, collaborating and confronting

In this method, persons involved in a conflict or having a difference of opinion, come forward to discuss the problem at hand with an open mind. They focus on resolving the conflict and finding the best alternative/solution for the team. They discuss by rising above personal emotions, with the sole intention of finding what is best for the team. This leads to a win-win kind of an outcome. Here everyone collaborates.

Although it sounds quite simple, the technique requires a certain level of maturity in the people involved.

Compromising/reconciling

In certain conflicting situations, there will be a need for the involved parties to think of a via-media wherein all parties decide to give up something and identify an acceptable resolution. Such solutions are often temporary in nature and can lead to a lose-lose kind of an outcome as the parties may feel they have lost something.

Withdrawal/avoidance

In some situations, one of the parties in the conflict may decide to retract from the discussion or decide to completely avoid the conflict by maintaining silence. This works well in situations where one of the parties in the conflict is emotionally charged up or angry. Hence, avoiding any conflict resolution provides a "cooling off" period so that the team can later come back for a meaningful resolution.

Forcing/competing

In some situations, a person with authority and power forces his/her opinion and resolves the conflict without giving any chance to others. This typically leads to a win-lose kind of an outcome. Someone may end up feeling like a loser while the other person with authority may feel s/he is a winner. This technique can be used if we see the conflicts are unnecessary and mostly destructive for the team.

Smoothing/accommodating

This technique is used when the atmosphere seems to be filled with apprehension/distrust among the parties involved. In these kinds of scenarios, one of the parties can take charge and try to ease out the situation. This can work as a catalyst to solve the discomfort between the involved parties by creating a feeling of trust and encourage them to come forward and resolve the conflict.

One should avoid taking conflicts personally. For example, if the boss states that you have done something wrong, it is best to segregate business and personal relationships and not assume that you are being criticised because the boss has a problem with you personally.

It is quite clear that women see and handle conflicts quite differently than their male counterparts. Conflicts have been found to affect women more, perhaps due to their higher sensitivity. Rather than the conflict, it is the perception of the conflict that affects them more. Conflict handling sometimes results in damages to interpersonal relationships. It is seen that men can overcome the damages to a personal relationship much quicker than women.

Work pressures, deadlines and excessive workloads

Several activities, projects and assignments come with deadlines. Delivering high quality work within the allocated time is the crux of building a strong and good reputation at work. According to several surveys, the deadline is the most common source of anxiety, which in turn leads to work stress and pressure.

Fig. 3 - Work deadlines (Illustration from Piaxabay)

Bosses and managers often love to use quotes like "the greatest inspiration for me is the deadline" or even "I know, you work much better under pressure". However, the fact is, normally people under pressure do not work better, they can at the most work faster!

Nevertheless, one is required to develop the capability to work under pressure and be able to meet the deadlines as both are inevitable. In fact, it is a very desirable quality to have and most of the job interviews include this as an assessment criterion. Not just in jobs, but in any profession that one takes, it is imperative to effectively deal with deadlines and work pressures.

Developing the ability to handle deadlines

Some of the simple and disciplined approaches help in developing the right skills and abilities as given below.

Planning and prioritising activities

Work baskets often get filled before we can even realise. To be able to finish all the tasks, one requires systematic time management tools. They help segregate activities based on their urgency and importance. Eisenhower's matrix (4 quadrant model) is ideal in self-help and the development of a time plan. Eisenhower matrix (Fig. 4) has 4 quadrants, each one representing the buckets for various activities based on urgency and importance.

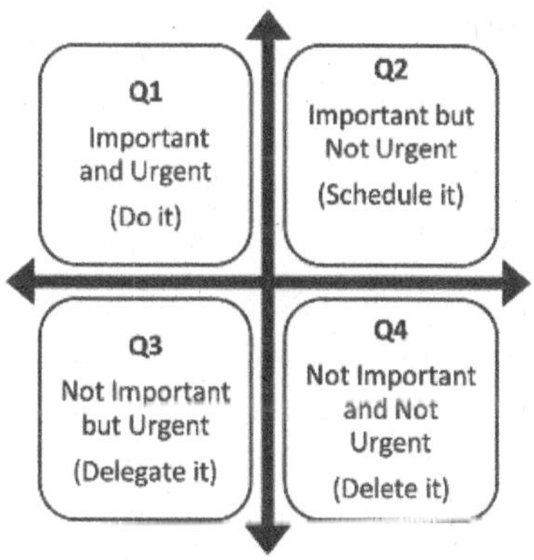

Fig. 4 - Eisenhower's Matrix

Eisenhower's concept of scheduling activities was beautifully expanded by Stephen Covey in his book *The Seven Habits of Highly Effective People*. According to these experts, Q1 activities need immediate attention (such as project deadlines, attending patients, answering customer complaints, handling breakdown maintenance, etc.).

However, these activities being intense in nature, they tend to consume all the time available at hand. As a consequence, a person is not left with any time to attend to the other important things, which fall in Q2. Since Q2 activities are important but not urgent, it is human tendency to turn to other urgent matters and thus prioritise Q3 after finishing Q1 tasks (not important but urgent). This shift of priority based on urgency rather than on the basis of importance is quite peculiar!

Q3 is often filled up by urgent matters wherein urgency is created by others (such as last-moment assignments, work pushed by colleagues, and lapses in planning) and hence where appropriate, these tasks could be delegated. According to Stephen Covey, Q2 is the Quality Quadrant, which helps in personal and professional development (such as acquiring new skills, fitness schedules, strategic thinking) and one should schedule these activities, lest important activities get neglected initially and create urgency or even a crisis later.

Q4 essentially includes all such activities that are time-wasters (like social networking sites, gossips, procrastination, and such) and should be altogether avoided.

This tool is highly effective in classifying the tasks correctly, placing them in respective quadrants and allocating adequate work time for each.

Asking for help/support

Stress is reduced if it gets shared with colleagues, bosses, and work friends. They can extend a helping hand in specific situations. It becomes critical how the communication in such cases is done while seeking help/support. Deadlines are manmade and not cast in stone! It also may be helpful to seek revised deadlines in case of genuine roadblocks.

> **"Having someone help you doesn't mean you failed. It means you are not alone!"**

Adopting mindfulness techniques

It greatly helps if the right mindset is developed to bear the work pressure. A few simple steps greatly help in improving the mindset. Some of them include taking breaks, being realistic while making commitments and finding positive actions to minimise stress.

Breaks can work miraculously! I myself have experienced it. I was under extreme stress during one of the critical projects. I was not able to find a way out on some technical matter and the deadline was approaching fast. Out of sheer frustration, I came home and tried to relax. That day, I slept unusually early. My mind was quite disturbed, so I did not sleep well that night. But to my surprise, when I woke up, I felt much better and peaceful. In fact, when I resumed work in the laboratory the next day, one bright thought came to my mind. I tried it out and Bingo! the solution fitted in, just like a missing piece of a jigsaw puzzle!

Haven't we heard the story of Kekule, the German Organic Chemist? He was said to have a great ability to visualise in the mind's eye, the complex images of organic molecules. He was unable to solve the puzzle about the structure of the Benzene molecule. On one occasion, he was partially asleep and dreamt (or visualised?) of a snake circling by holding its tail. This gave rise to the closed chain model of Benzene to be famously called Benzene ring later.

Developing good habits

We sometimes tend to forget what our parents taught us as children. Getting good sleep and rest is a simple trick that works miraculously in combating work stress. A clean and well-organised workplace helps the brain to organise its processes and data handling. Cluttering is no good inside the brain or in the outside space. Clutter at the workplace has an adverse effect on work efficiency.

Similarly, keeping good health and tenacity to work long hours also come as big assets. Personal health (physical, emotional as well as mental health) is the foundation of a person's ability to bear stress.

Cross-culture workplaces

Understanding cultural diversity is the key in modern life. Culture encompasses religion, food, clothing, language, social and religious beliefs and many more things. Employee cultural diversity sometimes creates barriers in the workplace. It is important to be aware of the differences and take extra efforts to accommodate such differences. Employing diversity training is one of the effective ways to change the organisation's outlook towards diversity.

Libya in the days of Gaddafi was opening the floodgates for skilled personnel and highly specialised professionals like medical doctors. The country, which had almost a cent percent

Muslim population, was a very conservative and traditional society. Social norms often made women wear traditional hijab/burqa, that too where only one eye could be visible! In the early 1980s, Dr Vilas shifted to Libya with his wife Anju and infant son Saleel to take up a job. With his quick learning of Arabic, his fair complexion and distinguished looks, Dr Vilas was easily accepted and respected in the city of Misrata. The locals would often take him as an Egyptian! With a funny working schedule of a 7-day day shift, 7-day evening shift, 7-day night shift followed by 7 days off, his working days would be quite busy. On average, 70-80 patients per day would be his workload. Many of the patients would be burqa-clad women. Visiting a doctor for health reasons would be their pastime! They would make up health-related excuses to freak out and engage in long chats with the doctors! One can imagine how doctors there must have managed their patients without getting into any trouble socially!

Helplessness and victimisation

Staying motivated and being supported by colleagues, managers, and bosses is a blissful state. We do not realise its importance and value until we find ourselves helpless and victimised. Helplessness on account of local politics, power-play, jealousy, gender discrimination, nepotism, favouritism, and many more human vices is not uncommon. Victimisation is a term often used to describe treating someone unfairly, because of their race, sex, beliefs, etc. Or it could be due to the prejudices created by specific actions of that individual against a colleague, senior, management, or organisation.

Unless organisations have a strong and supportive mechanism for redressal of individual problems, the situation may go out of control and the individual may go through emotional trauma. Women in fact are more susceptible to developing the feeling of helplessness and victimisation and there is a greater likelihood of them feeling distressed.

Usually, the first stop for many employees when they find themselves in an unresolvable situation is their immediate supervisor or manager. As a next step, they choose to go to the

HR department and as a last resort, to the top management. Any escalation therefore, is an indication of the ineffectiveness of the previous stages. The feeling of helplessness and victimisation is more predominant among the weaker levels of the workforce, including minorities and persons with reduced abilities. It is therefore the responsibility of every management and leadership to develop the workplace and more so, the work culture to minimise such possibilities. Developing a greater sense of employee empowerment at all levels and organisational ownership are the right approaches.

Aruna, who hails from Gujarat, is a computer systems professional having more than 3 decades of work experience in India and the USA. She told me how she had struggled to shape her career in the 1980s and '90s. She narrated an incident that happened 2 decades ago, making her as helpless as a caged cat. At that time, riding on the Y2K wave, she was venturing out to get a good lucrative job in the USA. She had done her homework well, acquired the right skills, applied at an Indian-origin company and all this at her own expense. With her supportive husband Anuj, she had cleared all the hurdles like getting the visa, arranging travel passage, and also getting the appointment letter from the company. The family was all set for her to leave for the USA while Anuj was to stay back in India with the kids, at least initially. All of a sudden, Aruna got a call from the officer-in-charge that she should appear for the last interview in person in Mumbai. In a hurry, just 5 days before her scheduled departure, Aruna and Anuj made urgent arrangements to travel to Mumbai and reach on time at the said place, which happened to be a starred hotel. It was their first-ever visit to such a posh place and while Anuj waited in the lobby, Aruna was required to go up. As she entered the designated place, she realised that it was just a guest room and not a conference room or a meeting room as anticipated by her. It was too late to retrace her steps. She went ahead. She was greeted by the officer-in-charge of the company. He was alone in the room. Aruna was directed to take a seat and he asked her to write down answers to a few irrelevant questions, which further raised her suspicion. He then made advances to her, and she gathered her courage and exited the room! A highly disturbed Aruna later discussed with Anuj what she should be doing. Shortly, she received an email from the officer-in-charge stating that if she went to the USA, the office would no more be able to support the job.

Aruna was helpless and agitated, having spent huge resources, a considerable amount of money, and time in getting the appointment letter, visa and tickets. With great courage, she decided to continue with the travel plan, and be mindful of the wicked, dangerous man and his misdoings. With some difficulty, she ultimately managed to reach the foreign land. The company did finally honour her appointment letter and she completed the assignment without any more trouble.

Many job seekers often find themselves in helpless situations and only those who gather the strength and are fortunate, come out of such situations without getting into deeper troubles.

Insufficient infrastructure/lack of good facilities

People spend most of their time at the workplaces, which could be 8-10 hours of the day or even more. It is, therefore, important for the company to focus on the biggest asset, that is the workforce, which is most affected by the infrastructure. The morale of the employee can be greatly impacted by the workplace environment. Performance and efficiency at work are closely linked with the office environment. New enterprises have a good opportunity to create the appropriate infrastructure, facilities, and environment. Old establishments are often challenged with upgradation needs. In the industry and service sectors, there are specific requirements related to occupational health and safety.

The healthcare sector, transport sector, especially the government/state-run facilities face great challenges in the creation, maintenance and upkeep of the right infrastructure. The employees and staff in these important sectors are therefore extremely stressed and could have very low morale at the workplaces.

Uncertainties

The workplace is full of uncertainties. Businesses undergo cyclic changes, new bosses take over, teams are abandoned, salary cuts are announced, new projects are about to be sanctioned, clinical trials are unsuccessful, and so on. Most individuals are unable to see the complete picture of the changes that are happening around them.

Chaos and uncertainty are nerve-wracking and even the toughest of the tough can buckle down under them. Accepting the craziness sometimes helps in safeguarding individual interest. The unpredictable economy is not a new phenomenon. If we were to believe the theory of Equilibrium, new norms get set and one is required to realign. In many situations, we can try taking up something entirely new, which helps in creating positivity and a sense of purpose, and gives a good direction to move on in the perceived uncertainties at work.

Since the outbreak of the COVID-19 pandemic, the world has witnessed an unprecedented wave of uncertainty. Many businesses have closed, many people have become jobless, and the economy has hit the rock bottom. When survival is at stake and life has seen an entirely new dimension of uncertainty, the human race will struggle for a new equilibrium. Corporates have struggled to sustain their businesses in the new normal. They have embraced technologies to stay connected at work, learnt to optimise resources, hoping for the best.

But what about individuals? Many have already lost their battles with personal health; many more have lost their employments and are struggling frantically. Those, who could plan and execute alternative activities, locations, skills, jobs, businesses, have better chances of revival and in turn, better chances of survival.

References:

1. Which are the best techniques for conflict management (knowledgehut.com)
2. Resolving conflict at the workplace, according to female CEOs (Karen Tietjen)
3. 'Female leadership trust advantage' gives women an edge in certain situations (22 June 2020, Science Daily)

Chapter 4

Organisational Framework to Handle Gender Equality

Gender equality

Fig. 1 - Gender equality (Artist- Durga Tilak)

Human Development (2019) Report says that out of 189 countries, India ranks 129th in gender equality! The World Economic Forum has also concluded with a similar number on the Gender Gap Index. India appears to be below even our small neighbouring countries like Sri Lanka, Bangladesh, and Nepal. The Gender Gap is often calculated based on 4 key areas, health, education, economy, and politics. Further, there is a sharp decline in the labour force participation of women (27% in the year 2018-19) and is much less than the world average of 48.8%.

The subject is too vast for a detailed analysis here. The data however should trigger various actions in the planning of careers.

Lack of infrastructure

Infrastructure for the workforce is found to be inadequate, inappropriate, or under-developed. The problem is further amplified because the infrastructure by itself is often not gender neutral. Hence, there are huge gaps that affect women disproportionately. Despite several years of progress, the gaps are disappointingly wide.

Let us take the example of Transportation. India's female labour force participation has always been among the worst in the world and had hit a new low of 23% in the year 2017-18. Apart from the contributing factors (for this diminishing figure) like education, culture, labour policy, etc. weak transport infrastructure is another important factor. All these aspects result in women choosing their jobs closer to their homes, which may often lead to compromises in their jobs and eventually careers.

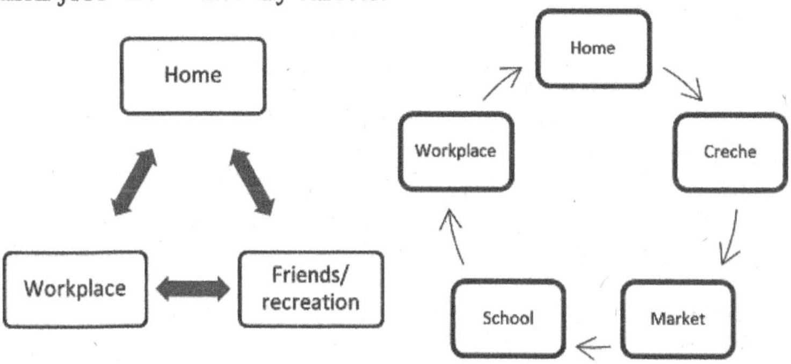

Fig. 2 - Transportation needs of (1) Men and (2) Women

As seen in Fig. 1, a woman's travel pattern is quite different from that of a man in an urban area. A woman's trip is often characterised by a chain of movements. Women make shorter and more trips, which often require them to change, divert, and break their journeys to pick up children, run errands, shop, or carry out other family obligations. This often makes transportation cumbersome, costly and time-consuming for women. In rural areas, the situation is quite peculiar.

Women are often overrepresented as "informal workers", and it is not surprising that their specific requirements related to transport are hardly addressed by transport planners.

Women are thus more affected than men when the access to employment, education or basic services is located far away from their residences. While citizens often prefer to use personalised mobility in towns and even metros, there is also a large dependency on public transport. According to the National Sample Survey

Office (NSSO), more than 60% of rural and urban households use the bus as their main mode of public transport, followed by autorickshaw, taxi, railway, cycle-rickshaw (NSSO 2016) and a very small percentage of personal mobility solutions like cars, two-wheelers and bicycles.

In many cities, the informal public transport system carries more passengers than the formal system. Affordable but poor quality of vehicles, unverified drivers and conductors, unpredictable schedules and a lack of accountability characterise the unregulated informal transport sector. Women from lower income group use slower and inexpensive modes of transport to manage transport costs, which worsens their time poverty.

Sexual harassment has a great effect on women's mobility, accessibility, and confidence. Lack of safety and security in public spaces and public transport affect women's human rights and their ability to participate equally in economic activities. There have been several studies conducted in India over the past few years that have explored the nature and extent of sexual violence that women and girls face in Indian cities, specifically in public spaces including public transport.

"Just because I am in a public place does not mean my body is a public place!"

Fig. 3 - Public places, unsafe places (Artist- Durga Tilak)

Women and girls thus fear using public transport because of violence and the fear of violence. In crowded public transport vehicles, women face harassment because the crowd offers anonymity. This has led to interventions such as "women only" carriages in metro trains or "women only" buses. Consequences of the violence and insecurity that women face lead to forced immobility. Simultaneously, women and girls are subjected to forced mobility when they are required to undertake trips, which are often unsafe because of the lack of services, such as water and sanitation.

A National Association of Software and Services Companies (NASSCOM) study showed that the female employees in the IT sector across India depended heavily upon the transport provided by the company as it was considered safer than public transport.

Providing safe transport

In India, women's concerns in urban transport came to the fore primarily through the lens of safety since the December 2012 Nirbhaya case. The incident brought the matter at the national level to urge the creation of a safer public transport system for women. The Government of India created the Nirbhaya Fund (during period 2013-16) to implement schemes for improving women's security. Setting up of a unified system at the national and state levels (City Command and Control Centre) for Global Positioning System (GPS) tracking through emergency buttons and video recording in public transport vehicles was planned in 32 cities.

In 2016, Maharashtra introduced the Tejaswini buses, which were ladies' special buses plying during the peak hours with women drivers and conductors. Numerous initiatives are underway such as reserved seats for women and ladies' special buses, coaches, and trains at the city level. However, these are not undertaken in a systematic or comprehensive manner.

An interesting case study is about Priyadarshini Taxi Service. It is an initiative by Susilaben Shah, a noted social activist and entrepreneur. Realising the gap in providing female-driven taxies in Mumbai, she started Priyadarshini Taxi Service. Women, whose earnings are less than ₹10,000 per month, are trained and employed to drive taxis (cars and autorickshaws). Over 50 women are a part of the service and many Priyadarshini women are sole bread earners of families. They are available 24x7 and guarantee safe travels to female passengers.

I have used their taxi service on two occasions for hotel drops during late-night international flight arrivals. On one occasion, the driver was an experienced one and knew the Mumbai suburbs quite well. Sitting in the co-driver's seat was an apprentice girl. She came from a small town in Maharashtra in search of livelihood. The senior one was giving her travel tips and other useful tricks of the trade, including advice on carrying a set of vehicle spares. I was extremely impressed by the self-empowerment and camaraderie shared by both the young lady drivers. At the end of my trip, I asked them if I could be of any help to them and the senior one said with benevolence, "Madam, please encourage all your lady colleagues to use our safe service!"

So here I am, urging all of you to spread the good word! To avoid the horrendous ordeals faced by Nirbhayas in metro cities, the Priyadarshinis offer safe transportation at late hours.

Facilities for expectant and new mothers

A NASSCOM HR survey indicates that a whopping number of female employees drop out at the age of 30 to 35 on account of their personal commitments and inability to get support from their employers. This creates collateral damage! A break in the job takes its toll on the career of women and on the other side, the employer loses precious and trained human resources. Another research survey carried out for this book indicated that more than 60% of respondents expressed that childbearing and raising the family was the most difficult phase of their careers. A majority of these respondents were women but there were quite a few men too. All of them expressed similar difficulties.

Employers are getting more and more mindful of these challenges faced by employees. To encourage more parents (especially mothers) to join and remain in the labour force, reliable, affordable, and good quality childcare is essential. Everyone from large corporates to the budding start-ups has started realising the significance of planning and investing in well-thought-out schemes, policies, and facilities to help women return to their workplaces after pregnancy and childbirth. Suitable creche development is an important aspect of the expanding infrastructure of many good corporates.

Fig. 4 - Crèche, an important facility (Illustration from Pixabay)

In the informal sector, the problem gets further multiplied. Just take an example of domestic workers (mainly women), who find it extremely challenging to manage their small children and their work schedules. I have experienced that if they get the flexibility of bringing small children to work, both the child and the mother remain quite peaceful and contented. This helps in more efficiency and better output. It is a matter of understanding and it changes the life of another person. The lady of the house can be a saviour for another woman, who is struggling to empower herself!

Legal enablers

International data published by the ILO and United Nations indicates that the gap between men's and women's labour force participation is more than 26%. This is particularly contradictory to the fact that women spend 2.5 to 3 times more time and effort in giving unpaid care and domestic work than men! In the Indian situation, the related statistics are further discouraging and lopsided. The first step is to examine how current laws provide the enablers. The next and more important step would be to identify the gaps that can be filled to nurture the participation of women in the workforce. With the progressive legislative scenario, there are several legal enablers in India. Some of the significant ones in the organisational context are enumerated below.

It is however incredibly significant that out of the total working population of Indian women, hardly 4.5% in the age group 15-50 years work in the formal sector! The framework therefore should be seen from a limited perspective.

1. Shop and Establishments Act/Factories Act, 1948

The basic act and amendments thereof address specific provisions like:

a. Toilets and clean washing places for women: The Act makes it obligatory for the shop/factory to provide and maintain an adequate number of latrines, urinals and washing places separately for men and women. The Act also empowers state government to specify the number. In reality, the situation is far from being satisfactory. Much has been talked about and written on this important but neglected area. Workplaces for many years have been conventionally designed by keeping the male workforce in view. It comes as no surprise that basic amenities such as clean and appropriate toilets in adequate number for women is a crying need at the workplaces.

b. Prohibition of work at hazardous places: The Act prohibits the employment of women in dangerous workplaces. I have come across situations where women themselves have sought permission to be working away from hazardous or dangerous locations and the organisations have enabled such possibilities without prejudice. The intent of the law is quite clear, and women can learn to protect themselves under these provisions.

   Safety at work is the right of women as well as men. Women should therefore ensure that this provision is not misused or misrepresented to avoid certain responsibilities. The places, activities and duties that otherwise are considered safe and appropriate for men should also be open for women!

c. Provisions for creche are required to be made in case the number of women employees is more than 30. This provision is further reinforced by Maternity Benefit (Amendments) Act, 2017.

   In some good organisations, creche facilities that are initially created for the benefit of female employees are also made available for male employees. This has greatly helped men to partake in raising infants.

d. Prohibition of night work: The law prohibited the appointment of women in other than general (daytime) shifts in the factories.

In the changing scenario, for bringing parity, there were several longstanding demands to amend the Act. Accordingly, the Amendment permits women to work on the night shift, provided the employer ensures adequate safeguards in occupational health and safety, equal opportunity for women workers, protection of their dignity and honour, their safe transport, etc.

2. Maternity Benefit Act, 1961 and (Amendment) Act, 2017

Maternity Benefit Act, 1961 makes quite important provisions such as:

- Prohibiting certain types of work during a specific period
- Payment of maternity benefit
- Payment of medical bonus
- Grant of maternity leave
- No deduction of wages
- Nursing breaks

Fig. 5 - Women and maternity benefits (Artist- Durga Tilak)

With time, there was a social need to amend some of the provisions. In line with the demands from various quarters and recommendations of the national labour conferences, the Maternity Benefit Act 1961 was amended, and these amendments came into force in the year 2017. In view of this, several positive steps are taken towards giving benefits to women during their employment. Major benefits are given below:

a. Increase in the maternity leave from existing 12 weeks to 26 weeks for working women having less than two surviving children. This is a very substantial benefit. Because 26 weeks is a good time for both, the mother and the child, to handle the changes that come with the mother resuming duty.

b. Extending maternity leave benefits for "commissioning mother" (in case of adoption and surrogacy) from the date the child is handed over. With the changing social needs, this is a very pragmatic step in supporting women in their personal decisions.

   At my previous employment, I came across one such application for maternity leave benefit by a commissioning mother. This came before the 2017 Amendment in Act came into force. However, going by merit, we decided to grant the benefits to the applicant, under the discretionary powers of the management.

c. Provision of permitting Work from Home facility for nursing mothers is of importance to young mothers and even fathers. With the forced changes in the work style necessitated by the COVID-19 pandemic, many such possibilities have opened. Not just the office environment, but medical services through teleconsultation, digital marketing, skilling sessions through digital platforms and many more are examples of this paradigm shift.

d. Mandatory provision for establishments having 50 or more employees to have the creche facility. The earlier limit of 30 female employees or more is now shifted to 50 employees or more. In addition, there is some flexibility related to the establishment or use of the shared facility. This amendment makes the provision more practical and increases the chances of deployment.

e. Nursing breaks in addition to the normal rest breaks. Women can often combine the breaks and utilise the facility as per their requirements. This amendment, in fact, is not known to many employees as well as employers and hence is not fully utilised.

f. Payment of medical bonus - A sum of 1000/- is the amount specified in the Act. This provision also has not been fully deployed.

The Maternity Benefit Act and its 2017 amendments are aimed at enabling the organisations/employers to establish a conducive atmosphere for women to successfully return to their jobs after a maternity break. The effectiveness of the Act greatly depends on the joint efforts by employees as well as employers.

Although the Act and its provisions are equally applicable for the unorganised or unregistered workforce, extending the benefits to these sectors is a big challenge.

3. Sexual Harassment of Women at the Workplace — Prevention, Prohibition, and Redressal

Fig. 6 - Sexual harassment at workplace (Artist- Durga Tilak)

Prevention of Sexual Harassment at the Workplace is a particularly important aspect in a society like ours that is opening new opportunities for women. The Sexual Harassment of Women at Workplace (Prevention, Prohibition and Redressal) Act 2013 (POSH Act) was enacted as comprehensive legislation to provide a safe, secure, and enabling environment, free from sexual harassment to every woman.

The last decade has seen fundamental and transformational changes in the Act that enables organisations to build workplaces and work cultures that are not just conducive but aim to welcome women's participation at all levels.

Background of POSH Act

The Constitution of India recognises the fundamental rights of individuals and Articles 14 and 15 of the Constitution give women their right to equality. Article 21 on the Right to Live gives women the right to live with dignity. Article 19 (1) (g) on the Right to practise any profession, trade, occupation/business gives women the right to a safe environment, which is free from harassment. Despite these provisions that have been clearly laid out in the Indian Judiciary, social injustice to women is rampant in Indian society.

Hon'ble Supreme Court of India in its landmark judgement in the year 1997 (Vishakha Versus State of Rajasthan Case) reiterated that these rights of women paved the way to an entirely new perspective and identified the need for guidelines to fill in the legislative vacuum.

It was much later in 2012-13 that the Indian Parliament passed the Sexual Harassment of Women at Workplace (Prevention, Prohibition and Redressal) Act 2013 (POSH Act). This Act came into force in December 2013. The main objective of the Act is that no woman shall be subjected to sexual harassment at any workplace in India.

The enactment of this important Act in India, especially in the corporate world, has made a great positive impact to create better and safer workplaces for women. It is thus evident that women at all levels have welcomed this Act.

Salient features of POSH Act 2013

The Act defines Sexual Harassment as any unwelcome sexual behaviour of direct or implied nature such as:

- Physical contact and advances
- Request for sexual favours
- Sexually coloured remarks
- Showing pornography &
- Unwelcome physical, verbal, or non-verbal sexual gestures and conduct

The keyword here is "unwelcome sexual behaviour"! The behavioural patterns are often relative to persons, cultures, communities, age groups, demography, and such. Keeping this in view, it is important to note that what is unwelcome to one person may not be so to the other! This aspect is particularly significant at the workplaces where diversity is bound to exist and should be nurtured.

One recent case will drive home the point. Sagar was a General Manager in a big corporate set-up and had a large team reporting to him. The team included many men and a few young women. Sagar believed in keeping a personal rapport with his team members. In fact, maintaining excellent interpersonal relationships was one of his biggest strengths. One of his teammates was going through a strained relationship with her husband and suffered emotional stress which adversely affected her work. Perhaps sensing this, Sagar came forward to have a supportive dialogue with her. She would often open up and express her anguish to Sagar. Both sides found comfort in talking to each other on a personal level. However, inadvertently Sagar once crossed the line, or so felt the lady. According to her, he went personal and enquired about how and when she was planning to get her divorce, her stand regarding alimony etc. It so happened that she came from a different culture than Sagar. She found these queries quite unwelcome and moved a case against him for verbal misconduct and sexual harassment at the workplace!

The interesting aspects of the context underline how the discussion regarding alimony was blasphemous in one culture while it was a normal dialogue in another. Demography, cultures, idiosyncrasies and even the state of mind could give different perspectives to the definition of harassment.

Significant provisions of POSH

The Act provides a civil remedy to the complainant. It further defines the scope covered under the term "workplace" and it is quite exhaustive. It includes government-owned/controlled organisations, private sector organisations, hospitals/nursing homes, education/training institutes, sports complexes/institutes, dwelling places (in case of domestic workers) and many more. It is therefore evident that the Act intends to cover a wide spectrum of activities and demographics.

The workplace also includes any place visited by the employee during employment, including the travel! It is quite clear that during travels the vulnerability of women is much more than that in the somewhat protected office environment. I have come across several cases involving harassment of a lady by a colleague during international and domestic travels that involved work.

One of the cases was in the late '80s. Those were pre-POSH days and times were quite difficult for women to raise their voice against such advances by male colleagues. A young lady and her male colleague were posted together in Europe on a project for the tenure of a few months. The young lady could sense the trouble at the departure from the international port itself. The nagging and pestering continued for quite some time even after reporting to duty in a foreign country. She was a no-nonsense type of strong person. On her first opportunity she called back her boss from India and based on her telephonic request, the male colleague's posting was changed to a different location. We all back in India office were silent observers to this extraordinary situation and the ladies in the group secretly admired her for the courage that she had shown. That truly prevented the situation from getting out of control on foreign land.

Organisational requirements

Coming to the Act itself, it makes specific provisions regarding the duties of the employer. It necessitates the establishment of the Internal Committee (IC), its composition, roles, responsibilities, and powers. The Act further directs the establishment of the Local Complaints Committee (LCC) at the District Level to provide redressal and remedial actions for the cases arising out of complaints from aggrieved women.

The Act further details the procedural and administrative requirements in handling the complaint, directions about the enquiry by the IC and LCC, penal provisions and specific requirements of maintaining fairness and confidentiality in all the deliberations.

Provisions to deal with the false/malicious complaint

The Act also addresses the possible situations where a complainant misuses the rights given to the women in raising their voice against any misconduct/sexual harassment. In the instances where the relevant authority establishes that the complaint is false or is made with malicious intent, the complainant can be penalised as per the Service Rules.

Work-related review by the boss sometimes results in an unpleasant exchange of words. In the Indian context, bosses are not often particularly good and professional at giving feedback and the employee sees this as an accusation. In some instances, ladies wrongly classify this as sexual harassment and misuse the provisions of this Act. To remove these erroneous interpretations, it is extremely helpful to impart formal training on the subject along with relevant case studies. Work-related scolding by the boss may be classified as "bossing" or in extreme cases as "harassment"; it should not be interpreted by the employee as "sexual harassment" just because the employee and boss are of the opposite sex.

Often it is seen that the job of IC is quite different from all other mundane committees that are operational within big organisations. IC is required to handle complex personal problems in an extremely sensitive manner. The committee is required to maintain the right balance based on data and evidence so that the complainant's interests are protected without victimising the respondent.

Some Myths about POSH

Some misconceptions about the Act still prevail in society. Here are some myths and facts for the readers to ponder on the matter.

Myth 1: POSH law affords protection from sexual harassment only for women. So, organisations cannot have provisions to protect men or the third gender from sexual harassment.

Fact: While it is true that POSH law offers protection from sexual harassment for women, it does not prevent organisations from constituting a "gender-neutral" sexual harassment prevention policy. In fact, this will allow the organisation the authority to handle complaints of sexual harassment for all genders.

Myth 2: According to POSH law, sexual harassment is when a man harasses a woman.

Fact: Since the complainant is an "aggrieved woman", many believe that the 'respondent' who is accused of harassment, must be a man. According to the POSH Act, the respondent can be a man, a woman or a person of the third gender. So, an aggrieved woman can file a complaint of sexual harassment against a man, woman or a person of the third gender.

Myth 3: POSH law does not apply when working from home or when working remotely.

Fact: POSH Act defines workplace as "any place visited by the employee arising out of or during the course of employment, including transportation provided by the employer for the purpose of commuting to and from the place of employment". According to POSH Act, this makes "home" a workplace. So, POSH Act applies to remote workplaces as much as it applies when employees work from an office.

Myth 4: If my intention is not bad, my actions will not be considered sexual harassment.

Fact: POSH law states that any act or behaviour that is perceived as "unwelcome" by the woman is considered sexual harassment. So, it is the impact of the act that matters and not the intention behind the act. The impact of the act depends on how the act was perceived by the woman.

Myth 5: POSH law is not applicable to organisations with less than 10 employees.

Fact: POSH Act states that any organisation that has 10 or more employees should mandatorily constitute an Internal Committee (IC) to handle sexual harassment complaints. The number of employees determines the requirement to constitute the IC and has nothing to do with the applicability of the POSH Act. Irrespective of employee strength, POSH Act is applicable to all organisations.

Myth 6: For MNCs that are headquartered outside India, the company's global harassment prevention policy and grievance redressal mechanism would suffice. They need not constitute IC for their Indian employees.

Fact: According to POSH law, any organisation in India that has 10 or more employees, irrespective of whether they are headquartered in India or not, should mandatorily constitute an IC.

Myth 7: Under POSH law, only women who are employees of an organisation can file a sexual harassment complaint.

Fact: POSH Act clearly states that an 'aggrieved woman' means "in relation to a workplace, a woman, of any age whether employed or not, who alleges to have been subjected to any act of sexual harassment by the respondent". The aggrieved woman can be anyone who is an employee of the organisation or visitor or customer or contractor or interviewee. So, any aggrieved woman, whether employee or not, can file a sexual harassment complaint against the respondent.

Myth 8: There is no penalty or punishment for false sexual harassment complaints and testimony.

Fact: POSH law grants powers to IC to take appropriate action against the complainant and witnesses for false complaints and testimony. It is important to note that there is no provision in the POSH Act for monetary compensation for the respondent in case of a false complaint or testimony.

Impact on organisations

The establishment of the Act brought in quite a stir in the corporate world and other sectors. It took them quite some time to understand and deploy the provisions of the Act in letter and spirit.

The sensitivity of the subject often has resulted in the organisations initially fumbling, then taking a cautious and conservative approach and finally emerging to be confident to nurture the changes in organisational DNA. As a Chairperson of IC, I have witnessed these steps and was actively involved in deployment in my organisation. This transition happened when I had already completed more than 25 years of my career. The new provisions, the assurance that the Act brought to women, the clarity it figured in the minds of the employees was a great experience for me also. On the other side, it also had a "me-too" effect. I thought to myself, had this provision existed earlier, I could have found myself in better comfort at work and a less vulnerable position. It brought to me a string of instances where I had to suffer silently the emotional trauma of being a subject of men's unacceptable advances.

One of the specific survey questions to support the research in this book was "To what extent do you agree that organisations should have a formal policy on equal participation by women?" In response, more than 82% of respondents expressed that the organisations should have a formal policy to encourage equal participation by women.

4. Provisions related to female directors

This provision is a major step towards the empowerment of women in the corporate world. The second proviso to section 149 (1) of the Act makes it mandatory for every listed company in India to appoint at least one woman director on the board. This provision is further enforced vide SEBI listing agreement 2014. Notwithstanding this, it is interesting to look at the data at the national level. In May 2018, the SEBI said that each of the top 1,000 listed companies must have at least one woman independent director by March 2020. As of December 31, 2019, 977 of those top 1,000 companies had a woman director, and 835 of them had a woman independent director. On the other side, there are many companies which are unable to fill these vacancies. The percentage of the board seats held by women is merely 5%.

What could be the major impediments to reach the international benchmark? There is truly an extremely limited pool of competent female candidates to occupy the boards.

Several countries have taken very bold and forward-looking steps to welcome diversity at the board level. Norway is one such country, which in the year 2003 itself mandated that within 5 years, the listed companies must make provisions to achieve at least 40% representation for women in the boards. Several other countries like Germany, Belgium, France, Malaysia, Spain, etc. enforced similar laws. Countries like the USA, UK, Canada, Australia, Singapore, and many more do not have a gender-based quota at the board appointments.

Ample study reports and research documents are available worldwide which highlight the significance and advantages of having women representation on the board of directors. There is a well-established correlation between good corporate governance and women's participation in boards. Studies also show that diversity in boards leads to several advantages like:

- Strong financial performance
- Ability to attract and retain top talent
- Heightened innovation
- Enhanced client insight - Women directors are likely to be more in tune with women's needs than men, which helps to develop successful products and services. After all,

women drive about 75% of purchase decisions in developed economies like Europe and the USA!

- Strong performance on non-financial indicators
- Improved board effectiveness - there is a strong link between women's presence and corporate reputation. Several companies use gender diversity as their investment criterion.

Experts believe that companies with female directors deal more effectively with risks.

Non-statutory enablers

Organisational obligations and good practices

Participation of women at all levels in the organisations has increased substantially. How do the organisations address this legal obligation to make the workplace conducive for women and free of sexual harassment? Most of the organisations in the country, be it small or big, have recognised the need to change the work environment, work culture, and more so, individual mindsets.

Organisations are getting ready to fulfil the obligatory redressal mechanism to the women workforce to address their complaints. Apart from these legal obligations, they also deploy strong internal policies such as zero tolerance for violation of specified provisions. All these are essential but reactive measures. Still more encouraging are the proactive steps taken by corporates to enhance gender equality at all levels.

Complete transition to a stress-free and ethical workplace is not at all easy to achieve. It takes deep commitment and efforts at all levels and by every employee. Barring a few notable exceptions, it would take years for our country at the pan-India level to reach our objectives.

Changing scenario

Very recently, my attention was attracted to a piece of interesting news! Zomato, the food delivery chain has announced a policy on "Period Leave" for their women employees. While announcing the policy, Mr Deepinder, CEO said to ladies that at Zomato, they want to foster a culture of trust, truth, and acceptance. And with immediate effect all women can avail up to 10 days of period leaves in a year. He also recognised the fact that men and women are born with different biological needs and there should not be any shame or stigma attached to applying for a period leave. He said that men should not be uncomfortable with the female colleagues expressing that they are on period leave. It is a part of life and while men would not fully understand what women go through, they should trust them and support them.

It is indeed a significant step towards inclusivity in its true spirit.

Paradigm and mindset

For ages, women are perceived to be weaker than men. Weaker in various aspects like physical, emotional, psychological, financial, and so on. It is for this reason that special provisions are being made in the Law, corporate ethics, organisational regulations, and social behaviours to protect the so-called "weaker" workforce. Women however, should not unduly depend on the organisational setup and provisions of POSH. They must ensure to build themselves into strong human beings and protect themselves effectively. Sexual harassment is just one of the unwelcome instances they encounter in their jobs and careers. It is very essential to build strength in multiple ways to combat the situations, if need be.

Women, all set to make impact

Avani Chaturvedi, Bhawana Kanth and Mohana are first lady fighter pilots of the Indian Air Force (IAF). For Avani, Bhawana and Mohana, the sky has no limit! The trio was inducted into the IAF fighter squadron after the Government of India decided to open a fighter stream for women on an experimental basis.

In response to the survey question (In reality, are the gender neutrality policies practised in your organisation?) Flt. Lft. Avani Chaturvedi responded, "Yes it does! Minor ups and downs are very natural at this stage; they will fade away as the number of women increases in the workplace. There are different social and moreover, biological roles, of women in society as compared to men. So when women go through that phase, they understand the other women in a better way as compared to men. The only way to get over this is to enter more women in all fields".

It comes from those committed women who have made their mark and those organisations, who have enabled them!

The message is very loud and clear!

Building up strength

Hundreds of research papers and scholarly books are written about overcoming weaknesses. One interesting book by psychotherapist and author Ami Morin being *13 things mentally strong women don't do*. She explains that men and women build mental strength the same way - gender does not matter. Further, cultural pressures, societal expectations and the subtle differences in the way girls are raised, are just a few of the factors that encourage women in engaging in certain unhealthy habits. She then explains how strong women overcome these 13 unhealthy habits. It is of course important to focus on building mental strength. But it is also very effective to keep in view the typical factors that one must not do!

There is no over-the-counter magic potion to make a person strong! We often come across some magnificent women achievers from various fields who demonstrate their strength in different ways. See the separate chapter on Women Empowerment for the details. It is amazing to see how seemingly ordinary women have transformed themselves into strong personalities.

References:

- Women and Transport in India (A policy brief, December 2017-Institute of Transportation and Development Policy)
- The Factories Act 1948
- The Sexual Harassment of Women At Workplace (Prevention, Prohibition And Redressal) Act, 2013
- Report on Enablers for Women Empowerment at workplace in India (Deloitte)
- The Maternity Benefit Amendment Act 2017

Chapter 5

Sectoral Peculiarities and Opportunities

"The most important investment you can make is in yourself."

- Warren Buffet

With a thriving economy like India, we see opportunities being opened in new sectors every year. Keeping track of the sectoral policies and opportunities, enhancing skill levels to match the job profiles, and grabbing those opportunities hold the key to building strong careers.

Sectors of the economy and types of work profiles

India is the fastest-growing large economy in the world. For a clearer understanding of various sectors of the economy, it would be useful to see how economic activities and manpower utilisation get classified. The economy can be broadly classified into various sectors based on ownership, working conditions and nature of economic activities as explained in Fig. 1.

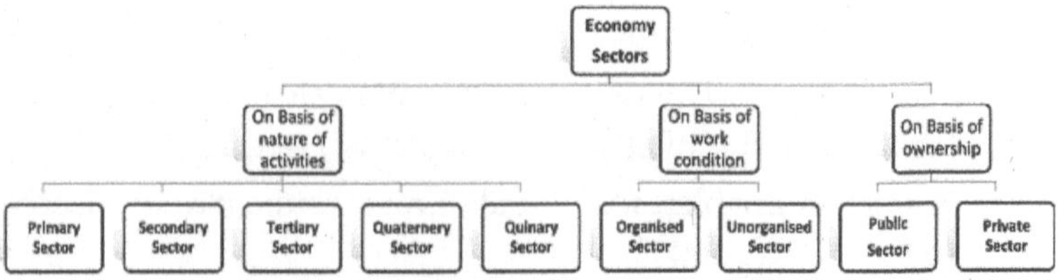

Fig. 1 - Simple classification of economy sectors

Primary sector

In the primary sector, activities are related directly to the utilisation of natural resources. Some examples of this sector are agriculture, mining, forestry, finishing, animal husbandry, etc. The primary sector is the backbone of early economic growth in civilisation. Due to the large dominance of agriculture, this sector is also known as Agriculture and the allied sector.

People engaged in this sector are called Red-collared because their activities are mainly related to fieldwork!

Secondary sector

This sector includes industries, where finished products are made from materials and resources obtained from the primary sector. Since this sector is associated with various industries, it is also called the industrial sector. Some examples are cloth mills, food processing units, factories producing chemicals, steel, plastic parts, automobiles, consumer goods, etc.

People engaged in this sector are often called Blue-collared.

It is worth noting that the collective performance of 8 core industries (electricity, refineries, coal, steel, crude oil, cement, natural gas, and fertilisers) is a strong indicator of the economic growth of the country.

Tertiary sector/service sector

The primary and secondary sectors need external support in many ways for enhancing production. This support is largely given by the tertiary sector. This sector is not directly involved in any primary or production activities but provides vital services like transportation, finance, banking, insurance, market access and several others. This sector is therefore also called the Service sector.

The people working in this sector are called White-collared. As the name suggests, the persons engaged in this sector work mostly in offices to handle desk jobs.

Funnily, the collar colours also expanded to have a gender-specific "Pink-collared". The term got evolved for professions that are conventionally handled by women. For example, doing babysitting, daycare, nursing, etc. It was also believed that the pink-collared jobs do not require any formal/professional training unlike the white-collared ones.

With the changing times, women are having easy access to white-collared jobs and men have started looking at pink-collared jobs certainly with a lot of respect.

As per the natural movement and growth, after the primary sector, the secondary sector flourishes and then the subsequent ones. It is interesting that in our case, our tertiary sector growth is much faster than our industrial sector. The recent GDP indicates that the service sector has contributed more than the industry.

Quaternary sector/Activities

Several "knowledge" and "intellectual" related activities of the economy from the tertiary sector are separated and classified as a Quaternary sector. Activities involving innovation, technology development, data generation and interpretation, education, skilling, theatre and art, hospitals, and clinics, etc. are covered here.

Quinary sector/Activities

There exists a level in the economy where important decisions are made. It includes governments, where legislation is done, top level industry leaders, who decide investment plans, high-level investors and financers, etc. The professionals working at this level of economy are often called Gold Collared. As the name suggests, they are highly skilled, highly paid government officials, industry leaders, researchers, legal/financial consulting services, etc.

Another term used with respect to economic growth is, sunrise and sunset industries.

Sunrise is a term used for a sector/industry, which is currently in infancy but has a very high potential for growth. On the other hand, sunrise industry can threaten already established industries, which have a high chance of rapid decline. Such an industry having very slim chances of survival, leave alone prospering, is termed as sunset industry.

Some significant sunrise industries are telecom, healthcare, information technology, infrastructure, retails, etc.

Sector-wise economic significance

Some significant facts of each sector are given below.

- The service sector is the largest sector of India. Gross Value Added (GVA) at current prices for the service sector is estimated at ₹96.54 lakh crore in 2020-21. The sector accounts for 53.89% of total India's GVA. India's rank is 8th in the world for the service sector.
- With GVA of ₹46.44 lakh crore, industry sector contributes 25.92%. India ranks 6th in the world in the industry sector.
- Agriculture and allied sector's share is 20.19%. India is the 2nd largest producer of agricultural products. India accounts for 7.39% of the total global agricultural output but we are way behind China.
- At 2011-12 prices, the corresponding contributions are slightly different (54.27%, 29.34% and 16.38% respectively).
- Sector-wise Indian GDP composition in 2017 was as follows:
    - o Agriculture (15.4%),
    - o Industry (23%), and
    - o Services (61.5%).
- Other contributing sectors
    - o Mining and quarrying: 1.63%
    - o Manufacturing: 14.43%
    - o Electricity, gas, water supply & other utility services: 2.7%
    - o Construction: 7.16%
    - o Trade, hotels, transport, communication, and services related to broadcasting: 16.42%
    - o Financial, real estate and professional services: 22.05%
    - o Public Administration, defence, and other services: 15.42%

Self-employment and entrepreneurship

Fast-growing India's young population is aspiring and future-oriented. However, the pace of skill development does not match that of technology in India, it never has. With more than 3 crore unemployed Indians seeking jobs now, the alternative being talked about is self-employment and entrepreneurship.

Self-employment is being increasingly recognised as one of the prominent ways of income in developing countries. It reduces the burden on job creation and encourages self-sufficiency with the use of minimal resources. India is witnessing a start-up boom across all sectors including technology, innovation, health, robotics, automobiles, food, education and so on. There are a total of 50,000 start-ups currently in India and as per the estimations, another 50,000 would be added by 2024!

To encourage budding entrepreneurs to kickstart innovative businesses that will eventually create employment opportunities, the government offers innumerable schemes and makes the process easy. Some of the prominent schemes being:

- Atal Incubation Centre (AIC), an innovation funding scheme was started by NITI Aayog in 2016. It is intended for students, researchers, or newly formed organisations in the fields of transportation, health, energy, education, agriculture, water, and sanitation, etc.
- NewGEN IEDC - In 2017, the Department of Science and Technology started the programme to promote knowledge-based and technology-driven startups through mentorship, guidance and support.
- MSME Market Development Assistance - Startups, Micro, Small and Medium Enterprises (MSMEs) can avail of this scheme to expand their activities.
- The Women Entrepreneurship Platform is launched by NITI Aayog for budding and existing women entrepreneurs.
- Micro financing scheme - National Minorities Development and Finance Corporation (NMDFC) provides financial (loan) assistance for NGOs and self-help groups.
- Swarojgar credit card - This scheme is beneficial for small artisans, micro-entrepreneurs, the service sector, fishermen, rickshaw owners, etc. It helps them in creating small working capitals.
- Venture Capital scheme for Agri-business development aims to promote agriculture development by providing market.
- Raw Material Assistance Scheme - The scheme helps in financing the purchase of indigenous and other raw materials.

- Pradhan Mantri Mudra Yojana - Under this scheme, loans are provided without the collaterals.
- Sustainable Finance Scheme- The scheme aims to provide financial assistance for sustainable development projects (such as renewable energy, green buildings, eco-friendly development, etc.)

Despite all these favourable schemes, entrepreneurship is full of challenges. It is quite motivating to see the success stories around us. In addition to emulating good practices, it is often essential to also look at the failures more closely!

Agriculture and the allied sector (primary)

Fig. 2 - Agriculture; an important sector (Illustration from Pixabay)

Agriculture is an important sector in the Indian economy. However, over the last few years, the contribution of the Agriculture sector to India's GDP is gradually decreasing. Despite this reduction in the share of GDP, this sector remains significant in another aspect, namely employment. Agriculture and allied activities take a large share of about 55% of employment. For many, agriculture and allied activities like animal husbandry are the way of life.

Role of women in agriculture

What is the role of women in agriculture? In fact, women play a significant role in the agro-based economy. It is often perceived that they perform less-skilled jobs such as sowing, transplanting, weeding, and harvesting, which fits well within their framework of domestic life and child-rearing.

The national data indicates that out of the total women population in the agriculture sector, about 33% are cultivators (working on their own/family lands) and about 67% are agriculture labourers (working on other farms for wages). With the migration of menfolk to the urban areas in search of jobs, women shoulder more and more responsibilities on the farms. In addition to managing the household with the bare minimum facilities, women take major responsibility for livestock and poultry. Livestock and poultry have traditionally remained responsibilities of women in any case.

In fact, when it comes to gender disparity, even developed economies like the USA and Canada have quite similar situations. A report on Canadian women farmers indicates that women carry out much more work on the farms as compared to their male counterparts. But when it comes to ownership rights, equal wages, access to capital, participation in decision making and many other important aspects that govern empowerment, women farmers are significantly at a disadvantage.

Major impediments for farming women

The barrier for women to participate in more skilled operations is also high illiteracy (estimated to be 60-65%). Moreover, a large number of them participate in agriculture work as unpaid workers. Thus, the rigorous work that they undertake is grossly undervalued. In fact, even the paid female workers get 30% less wages as compared to their male counterparts. Daughters in rural areas typically supplement or substitute their mothers' household work (obviously unpaid) and thereby lose the opportunity for schooling.

India's small landholding pattern has hindered the large penetration of mechanisation in farming. Still, with sustained efforts, India is standing at the level of about 40-45% of mechanisation in major farming operations. To give better access to women for mechanised farming equipment, there is a need to address their operational requirements. The majority of such equipment is designed keeping male farmers in mind.

SAE India (Society for Automotive Engineers) runs a student competition for designing mechanised farming equipment. Over the last 3 years (starting in 2019), the subject of the competition was to design an onion harvester. When the students started working on the designs, they quickly recognised that onion harvesting was primarily handled by women workers. Their designs therefore, were more focused on ergonomics, suitability, and applicability to women. These small efforts have started making a difference in the way facilities get created in the agriculture sector.

Women are often deprived of land ownership rights. Family-owned lands are passed on from generation after generation to only male children. Women therefore historically do not have any major say in financial decision-making, access to markets and such. Since women do not have ownership of land, they do not get benefitted from the government's subsidy schemes, credits, loans, capital, and other benefits.

Fig. 3 - Farm workers (Artist- Durga Tilak)

Lack of basic hygiene and healthcare in farming areas is a major national issue. The farming population is known to be exposed to a number of biological, respiratory, environmental and safety risks. Non-availability of clean, potable water, lack of sanitation facilities and ignorance add to the miseries. Excessive exposure to pollens, grain dust, livestock pests, fungal spores, etc. often results in lung diseases. The morbidity pattern among women workers reveals that their ailments were primarily due to poverty and occupation. Women in this sector are truly at the bottom of the social order.

There is a significant study available which indicates that a large number of farming women who do not own land, are subjected to physical violence and psychological abuse. Ownership rights have seen a dramatic decrease in violence!

Who will forget the epic film of 1957, *Mother India* portraying the exploitation of poor farmers, especially a woman, by a money lender? It also revolves around agrarian poverty and a woman's hardship as she tries to survive with children in the absence of her husband. Despite the overall progress made by the country in last several decades, the struggle of farming women still remains very real and very basic!

Secondary sector

The industrial sector is one of the main sectors that contribute to India's GDP. The industrial sector (that includes manufacturing, mining, and quarrying, and electricity, water supply, and gas sectors) accounts for around 23% of India's GDP.

Manufacturing Industry in India has gone through various phases of development since independence. The foundation of domestic manufacturing was laid in the 1950s and early 1960s. What is known as the Licence-permit Raj, shaped certain industries until the 1980s. After a phase of liberalisation in the 1990s and finally to the present phase of global competitiveness, the sector has truly seen transformations.

According to the recent statement by CII (Confederation of Indian Industries), the Indian manufacturing sector currently contributes 14 % to GDP and it is estimated that every job created in manufacturing has a multiplier effect in creating 2-3 jobs in the service sector. In a country like India, where employment generation is one of the key policy issues, this makes the sector a critical one to achieve inclusive growth.

While several factors like robust domestic demand, a growing middle class, a young population, and a high return on investment make India a credible investment destination and present an attractive opportunity to manufacturers, the Make in India campaign has emerged as a unifying factor with a holistic approach to take India to a new level of economic growth. The 25 strategic sectors that have been identified under the campaign offer a gamut of opportunities for investment.

Tertiary sector

The growth of the service sector in India is a unique example of leapfrogging traditional models of economic growth. From primary sector growth, the industrial/manufacturing growth is normally the next logical step. In the 70+ years since Indian independence, the lion's share of the contribution to the country's GDP has been made by the service sector. However, it still employs only 25% of the workforce.

The IT/ITeS and Fintech sectors have the potential to grow between 10-15% p.a. Exports form their largest component. Our key advantage has been a low-cost, but skilled and predominantly English-speaking workforce. Going forward, the IT and ITeS segments require significant upskilling to move to a 'high value add partner'. Indian IT companies can also leverage their skill sets to provide fintech solutions to global financial customers. Financial risk management services, insurance, engineering modelling are examples of high value add services performed within India for a global audience.

Technology, the sector, close to my heart, has a promising scenario when it comes to women's participation. According to NASSCOM's report, "India's technology industry has been growing its D&I mandate and this is evident from the fact that the industry boasts of over 35 percent women workforce at about 1.5 million, a growing number of Persons with Disability (PwDs) and LGBTQI+ are being onboarded and trained for operations and client facing roles. And this journey continues."

Tourism offers great growth potential. Availability of world-class medical facilities, skilled doctors, technicians, and pharmaceuticals are some of our advantages for medical tourism. With digital communication and interfaces, diagnostic medicine can also be tapped into as a service for global customers.

India is renowned for its places of natural beauty; thus, tourism has exponential possibilities to boost the service sector in the next decade. To make a global mark, improved customer experience (medical or tourism) is the key factor, in addition to better infrastructure facilities, safety, connectivity, etc.

Construction, infrastructure development and real estate are some of the fast-growing activities. For the length and breadth of our country, infrastructure development needs to accelerate to catch up with the demands of society. Huge opportunities exist in these areas for jobs as well as entrepreneurship.

Transport and logistics are seen as the next promising fields on account of rapid economic development. The logistics market in India is projected to grow at a CAGR of 10.5% between 2019 and 2025. E-commerce is another major segment that is expected to support the growth of the logistics industry during the forecast period. Port capacity is also expected to grow, thereby, adding a capacity for material handling. Indian Railways aims to increase its freight traffic to 1.1 billion tons in 2030. Freight traffic on airports in India has the potential to reach 17 million tons by FY 2040. However, lack of supporting infrastructure, automated material handling systems and skilled manpower, slow adoption of technology and high manual processes are some areas where the Indian air cargo industry needs to buck up as compared to its global peers.

Quaternary

Some important industries in this sector are knowledge and information management, media, entertainment, education, medical/hospital services and more. The Education field is a representative and significant contributor.

Educator and teaching careers

The contribution of women to education is extraordinary. Savitribai Phule (1831-1897) is the first female schoolteacher of 19th century India. It is often interpreted that the traditional role of a mother in their households helps women relate to students in schools. In fact, the ability to understand children's emotional needs better makes women a preferred choice at least for primary education. Also, women are good counsellors and their presence in schools enhances the sense of security. At higher levels, males appear to be a better choice, not because of their teaching skills but because of higher qualifications, more stress on discipline amongst students and other behavioural requirements. It is however, not appropriate to consider professionals better just based on their gender. Teaching is about imparting knowledge in the best way possible. As a teacher, one must be able to impart knowledge in such a way that it gets cast in the minds of students. Malala Yousafzai said it all: One child, one teacher, one book, one pen can change the world.

When it comes to employment in the education sector, contrary to common perception, more men are employed than women. Even though the profession continues to be preferred amongst women given that both school and college-level teacher eligibility examinations have more female applicants, it is the males who are getting more jobs as teachers across designations than women.

India has 2,05,339 more male teachers than females, according to the Higher Education report 2017-18. Of the total 12,84,755 teachers across India, 57.99% are males. The gender gap becomes wider as we move up the hierarchy, according to the data from the Union Ministry of Human Resource Development. The gender gap is, however, marginal in the case of contractual jobs.

Fig. 4 - Educator's role (Illustration from Pixabay)

While more men tend to hold higher positions, including that of associate professors and professors, when it comes to tutoring jobs, the number of women is double that of men.

The scene is worst in Bihar and Jharkhand where only 20.93% and 29.87% of teachers are females, respectively. Male candidates also dominate teaching in Maharashtra (39.76% females), Odisha (35.77% females), Telangana (38.38%), UP (32.84%) and West Bengal (34.58%).

In several developed economies, the trends are quite different. Women are considerably over-represented in the teaching profession. Recent data shows that among Australian university graduates, 97% of pre-primary teachers, 85% of primary teachers and 68% of secondary teachers are female.

Media and entertainment

The Indian Media and Entertainment (M&E) industry is a sunrise sector for the economy and is making significant strides. Proving its resilience to the world, the Indian M&E industry is on the cusp of a strong phase of growth, backed by rising consumer demand and improving advertising revenue.

Cinema, Television, Radio, Publishing, Music, Gaming, and the Internet open a wide canvas of options. The other business verticals like Advertising, Media Research, Public Relations, Corporate Communication and Media distribution support the media industry in its operations and executions. The jobs in the media industries are distinct, interest-specific and give job satisfaction with career growth and heavy pay packages.

The professionals are divided into Above-the-Line and Below-the-Line. Those who are working in a creative field like creative writing (script, dialogues, songs, feature writing etc), directors, art directors, cinematographers, actors and actresses, radio jockeys, singers, music composers and directors, lyricists, etc. are considered Above-the-line artists or professionals. Most of the Above-the-line professionals work on a project or assignment basis and can charge their professional fees as per their creative capabilities, experience and popularity. The professionals, who have technical expertise in handling camera, lights, studios, accounting, marketing, production, release, and distributions are considered Below-the-Line professionals. Most of the Below-the-Line professionals work in the media industry on salaries and their salary varies based on their role and expertise.

It is reported that less than 5% of leadership positions across media companies are occupied by women. The number stands at 13.6% for magazines, 20.9% for TV channels, and 26.3% for digital portals. Women are gradually making a mark in the media world playing various roles as reporters, writers, news analysers in print and broadcast media, anchors, compeers, and effective moderators in discussions. However, what is disheartening is the representation of women in media as sexual objects, skimpily dressed glamour dolls, vamps and other negative shades.

Participation of men and women in economic activities

2018-19 data indicates that in the rural sector, the Worker Population Ratio (WPR) was about 19% for females and 52% for males. In the urban sector, the ratio is 14.5% and 52.7% respectively. It gives a clear picture that female participation in economic activities is considerably lower than males.

Labour Force Participation Rate (LFPR) for male workers in age 15+ years had declined from 79.8% to 75.5% from 2011-12 to 2018-19. The ratio for female workers in the same age group also declined from 31.2% to 24.5% during the same period.

Coming to the wages, the disparity between male and female workers continues. The earning of a female worker is less than that of a male worker. These figures vary from state to state – it's the maximum in Lakshadweep and minimum in Dadra & Nagar Haveli. State wise too, similar trends continue. For example, in Lakshadweep, a woman's average wage is ₹121 per hour and man's wage is ₹131 per hour. In the UT of Dadra & Nagar Haveli, these figures are ₹31/- and ₹38/- respectively.

On the other hand, the data of time spent in various activities by men and women portrays quite a different picture. As per Time Use Survey Report 2019, on average, 299 minutes were spent in a day by females for "Unpaid domestic service activities for household members" against 97 minutes spent by males on these activities. Similar trends were observed both in rural and urban areas. Under the unpaid domestic services, females are spending major time on the activity "Food and meals management and preparation". Other activities include caregiving for elders, house maintenance/ cleaning, shopping, and household management, etc.

Fig. 5 - Household duties (illustration from Pixabay)

This reminds me of a very heart-warming childhood story, "Dinuche Bill" (Dinu's Bill in Marathi). It is the story of a young boy named Dinu who, on understanding what a 'Bill' means, presents his mother with a bill for the work he did the previous day. The mother pays the bill amount promptly. But then she also writes another bill in Dinu's name. The bill contains a list of all tasks that she had done to bring Dinu up through his birth and childhood. Only this time, each entry and the total amount stated in the bill is zero!

It is quite clear that men contribute more directly to economic activities and women, more indirectly. The previous chapters highlighted the need for equal participation. When women choose to increase their participation in the economic activity, the necessary support system to take care of their other burdens is imperative.

Creating more opportunities by skill enhancement

Learning opportunities should always be grabbed. In fact, one should never stop learning because life never stops teaching!

I have often experienced that formal education in schools and universities takes one at a certain capacity level and I would equate it with Potential Energy. Applying that education to develop relevant skills, right aptitude and directing it towards meaningful (economic or otherwise) activities, is like converting this potential energy to kinetic energy! The kinetic energy is what keeps one progressing towards one's goals.

Pradhan Mantri Kaushal Vikas Yojana (PMKVY) 2.0 is the flagship scheme of the Ministry of Skill Development and Entrepreneurship (MSDE). The objective of this skill certification scheme is to enable a large number of Indian youth to get industry-relevant skill training that will help them secure better livelihoods. The Short-Term Training (STT) is an integral component of PMKVY which enables candidates to undertake industry-designed, quality skill training for a period of three to six months, become employable and procure livelihoods. According to NSDC's Skill Database Management System (SDMS) data, till February 3, 2020, 33.6 lakh candidates had been trained and, of these, 15.3 lakh were reportedly placed (45.6% of the trained candidates).

This clearly highlights the fact that upskilling greatly enhances the employability of the candidates.

The analysis report by NSDC highlights that the gender, age and education of the candidate seem to be important factors in several sectors, but to a varying degree. In fact, several factors can influence sectoral performance. These could be external – such as the state of the economy, job creation, presence of the industry in the region, investment scenario – all of which influence placement prospects. Constraints on matching the supply of skills with their demand due to information asymmetries may affect placement rates as also the misalignment of training numbers with local demand.

Participation in decision-making

In addition to economic participation, one important aspect of gender parity is the participation in political decision-making. According to the reports, some interesting figures speak for themselves:

The representation of women in the Central Council of Ministers has declined over the years. The proportion of women ministers is less than 10% in 2020. A total of 78 women members, constituting 14% of the Members of Parliament (MPs) have been elected to the 17th Lok Sabha, the highest since independence. The highest number (11) of women MPs in the 17th Lok Sabha has come from Uttar Pradesh and West Bengal.

At the all-India level, the women representation in the State Assemblies was 11%. The highest women participation in Panchayati Raj Institutions was observed in the states of Rajasthan (56.49%), followed by Uttarakhand (55.66%) and Chhattisgarh (54.78%).

When it comes to the judiciary, the highest number of women judges is 10 in Punjab and Haryana High Court, followed by 9 in the Madras High Court. Some state high courts do not have any women judges!

The data on leadership positions in corporates is also indicative that the "Gold Collar" is still not easily accessible to women!

References:

- Indian Economy; An overview (Invest India Report)
- Women and Men in India 2020 (Report by Ministry of Statistics and Program Implementation, Government of India)
- Female work and labour force participation in India- A Meta Study (By UNDP)
- Pradhan Mantri Kaushal Vikas Yojana 2.0, Short Term Training (2021 Report by National Skill Development Council)
- India's Tech Industry: Women for the Techade (March 2020 Report by NASSCOM)

Chapter 6

Overcoming Stereotypes

"I think, women are foolish to pretend they are equal to men. They are far superior and always have been. Whatever you give a woman, she will make greater. If you give her sperm, she will give you baby. If you give her a house, she will give you a home. If you give her groceries, she will give you a meal. If you give her a smile, she will give you a heart. So, if you give her any crap, be ready to receive a ton of shit!"

- William Golding

What is a stereotype?

We often come across the term "stereotype," and it somehow carries a negative tinge! In simple words however, a stereotype means a fixed, over-generalised belief about a particular group or class of people. Others expect people belonging to that group to behave in a particular manner or pattern, which is the characteristic of the group.

While it sometimes helps in taking quick decisions based on stereotype characterisation, there are several disadvantages of a stereotype. The major disadvantage is that we tend to ignore differences in individuals and grossly depend upon generalisations. Stereotyping often leads to social characterisation, prejudices, and might lead to wrong conclusions.

Various stereotypes, such as racial, gender, cultural, national, social, ethnic, etc. are part of our day-to-day behaviours. So much so that the personal behaviours get embedded into social behaviours and are responsible for creating positive as well as negative impacts in the work environment.

Advertising, media, movies, literature, comedies, etc. are known for creating, maintaining, and further enhancing stereotypes. Haven't we heard innumerable Sardarji jokes, blonde jokes, Marwari jokes, more recently Alia jokes and such? These jokes are built around the stereotypes that certain communities/ people are dumb, miserly, morons and such. Hollywood and our own Bollywood movies portray characteristics of different cultures and diversities to fit into stereotypical categories. Similarly advertising and media create stereotypes of macho men and their most desirable object to be beautiful women. Stereotypes are also common in portraying women as "damsels in distress" or "Woh (The other woman)".

Stereotypes in professions

For generations, women are expected to be caregivers and men to be bread-earners and protectors. Later, when women started to move out of the four walls of their protected environment and take up jobs, career choices got to be perceived as "women's jobs" and "men's jobs". Gender stereotypes always hamper workplace diversity and thus limit the progress in many professions. Most affected are of course women but it does affect men too. Men are often ridiculed when they want to choose a female-dominated career such as nursing, teaching, classical dancing and likewise.

The root cause of these societal issues is often found to be in the families and close social circles. Many stereotypes are imposed on children by parents, teachers, relatives, and friends while they are growing up. Don't we buy toy cars for boys and dolls for girls? Children also learn from the fact that the number of stay-home moms is much more than stay-home dads. The stereotype gets developed that moms remain at home to take care of children and dads go to work because they must earn money for the house. There are several other stereotypes that family upbringing creates, whether intentionally or unintentionally.

Going back in time, I remember the childhood of my son, Sarang. I often created new games to engage him in fun-filled activities. On one such occasion, I introduced Sarang to "Role Play". So, accordingly, he was to be mommy and I would be Sarang. He immediately understood the play and we started off. He filled in the tiffin box for me, and I started messing around! Then he brought inside dried clothes and started folding them and I took up the art book to scribble on it. He then told me that mommy is going to the office for urgent work, and I should be a good girl and play at home. In his make-believe world, he took out a scooter, reached office and started work. I was amazed when he imagined "work" to be some physical activity and took out an imaginary tiller and started digging into the soil!

Fig.1 - Mommy goes to "work" (Artist- Durga Tilak)

I was speechless with his innocence. In the next few weeks, I made it a point to take him to my workplace, showed him around the laboratory and introduced him to my colleagues. I explained to him in simple words about my work as a Project leader. He loved every bit of it, so much so that later, whenever I had extra work on weekends, he would accompany me to the office. He would take his activity books, sit quietly or chat with everyone while I finished my actual "work"! To Sarang, it was an early introduction to the automotive world, which he later chose as his own area of expertise.

The "men's" and "women's" jobs

The jobs in the industry were traditionally considered to be "masculine". With the change in the job market, men started looking for different, more stable jobs like healthcare, teaching, catering, etc. If we look around, we hardly see ladies doing jobs like plumbing, electrical servicing/maintenance, car repairs/ servicing, food delivery, mail delivery and so on. Coming to the use of language, the European parliament in the year 2008 passed the regulation for the use of gender-neutral language. Many languages like English, German, French, etc. had to create new words to represent neutral professional titles for "midwife", "chairman" and many more.

I happened to visit Europe at that time and remember seeing a cartoon which showed a boy running home, and with all excitement yelling, "Mom, just saw a milk-person falling in a person-hole!"

The changes are happening, although slowly. Some career choices that have shown significant trends, speak for themselves:

- Nursing is a female-dominated category. In fact, it took many years to change the Oxford Dictionary definition to "a nurse is a person who gives care to the patient" from the earlier "a nurse is a woman...". The health workers data in India shows that the female to male ratio for nurses is about 80:20. It is however paradoxical that in general, male nurses earn more than female nurses, in a field that is female-dominated. Here is another stereotype that a man must earn more than a woman! The regulatory requirements like the Equal Wages Act and employment policies are trying to influence the equal wages requirements but informally, wage discrimination remains a glaring fact in this sector.
- Engineering is a male-dominated career choice. Studies indicate that the main reasons why fewer women opt for engineering are, fear of negative prejudice, lack of confidence and lack of motivation. Another major concern driving women to leave their engineering jobs midway is the workplace issues in a male-dominated field. In fact, the entire STEM (Science, Technology, Engineering and Mathematics) has always remained male-dominated. According to the United Nations, women constitute merely 14% of total scientists, engineers and technologists in R&D institutions in India despite them accounting for 40% of STEM graduates. Another revealing statistic says that India tops the world in producing female graduates in STEM but ranks 19th in employing them!

- In the case of educators, the provisional data from Unified District Information System indicates that in the country, there are about 95 lakh teachers in schools with men and women in about equal number. On the other hand, for higher education, the ratio of male teachers to female teachers is different (58% to 42%) and it differs in individual states. Bihar for example has a ratio of 75:25 while states like Kerala, Goa, Punjab, etc. have more women teachers than men.

International data shows that in countries such as Australia, the percentage is quite high (97%) for women teachers. The primary reasons for such a low percentage of men taking up teaching jobs are the traditional thinking that the teaching jobs are meant for women and more so, men prefer other jobs due to higher wages. These countries are therefore struggling to establish policies to attract more men and achieve the desired diversity in the sector.

Bosses

We see around the typical stereotype images: Men enjoy working on cars, they do not do household work, they are doctors, they play outdoor sports and video games, they like sports channels and outdoors, they are lazy and messy and above all, they are bosses!

On the other hand, women are presumed to have easier jobs, they are not as strong as men, they make less money than men, they love cooking and household work, they need to be protected, they like to look pretty and above all, they are bossy!

Fig. 2 - Stereotype: Male and female boss (Artist- Durga Tilak)

In the office, one day I received a telephone call. After hearing a female voice and then responding to my "Good morning!", he (the caller) requested to be connected to my boss. It so happened that I was the Director and top boss of the Institute, hence could not understand the question. I responded politely and asked whom he wanted to speak to. "To your boss, the Director", came the reply. Amazed at the stereotype that the secretary must be a lady and her boss has to be a man, I chuckled and clarified to the embarrassed caller that he could very well talk to me, since I was the Director!

Dr Sucheta, neuro-physician at Apollo Hospital, narrates similar experiences. Often during her OPD rounds in the hospital, she is accompanied by a junior male doctor. Invariably, the new patients address her as "Sister" and her junior as "Doctor". Patients somehow presume that the male colleague is the real "Doctor" and the accompanying lady is a nurse assisting him.

Women leaders

With these stereotypes about the boss, how does one deal with the boss? Normally, as the research clearly indicates, all things being equal, men and women can be equally effective or fit as bosses. However, they may have different leadership styles. Women are known to adopt coaching and mentoring styles and men demonstrate command, and control styles. This is also one of the stereotypes, but more to do with psychological and behavioural peculiarities as highlighted in Chapter 1. Some of the studies in the early '90s indicated that women's leadership is more effective in female-dominated settings and likewise, men are more effective as leaders in male-dominated or men-oriented settings. A relatively old analysis (in the year 2003) concluded that women are more likely to adopt a "transformational" leadership style than men. It is also reported that women have the following tendencies. While the list is neither exhaustive nor rigid, it helps in better understanding the lady bosses. Recent trends might reflect some behavioural changes, still the significant differences will always be there!

- **Task focused**

  Women leaders tend to be extremely focused on completing the assigned task. The task-oriented nature also results in the smooth running of operations on a daily basis. The followers sometimes may not clearly understand why the tasks are so important in the context of the strategic perspective. The leadership style thus gets questioned, and the leader is expected to handle such situations with firm but fair behavioural modulations. In management terminology, it is often seen that women leadership is more "tactical" in nature than "strategic".

- **Transformational leadership**

  As stated above, a number of studies indicate that women are more likely to adopt this style than men do. Transformational leaders work towards gaining the trust and confidence of the followers/team members and often establish themselves as role models. They also empower and encourage the followers to develop their fullest potential. Such situations prompt the individuals to contribute their best to the organisations. Transformational leadership is a powerful characteristic that enables the leader to change the current business model or business direction.

- **Preference for flat organisational structures**

  On many occasions, women prefer to lead or given a choice, create a flat type of organisations. They also prefer cooperation and collaboration within and amongst the teams. Collaboration and cooperation are intended at extracting the best from the teams. However, individual contributors and high performers may not get highlighted. Cooperation is also preferred to avoid creating an extremely competitive environment, which leads to stress for the team as well as for the leader.

- **Indirect communication**

  Women tend to communicate their expectations related to work/goals/tasks somewhat indirectly and allow more freedom to the subordinates to achieve the same. Greater freedom to the team/members to achieve the stated objectives empowers them and prepares them for higher or bigger roles. On the flip side, it hampers direct guidance or frank assessment, unless specifically sought by the members.

Also, on some occasions, the boss assumes or takes for granted that the same level of understanding exists with the subordinates and its absence might lead to disappointments and frustrations for the leader!

- **Mentoring and training others**

  Women leaders establish a personal rapport with colleagues and create stronger bonds. These bonds extend beyond work. They often advise and provide guidance beyond the work and help the members develop their own abilities.

  I am reminded of Mrs Meena Chandavarkar, a noted educationist in Maharashtra. She was the Principal of Abhinav Vidyalaya, a famous school in Pune and brought in great reforms in pre-schooling. She led her teaching and non-teaching staff with a great conviction and value that "Child is the centre of our world". She had a personal rapport with all the teachers, every child and even every parent! She would remember every child by name, his/her strengths and make it a point to talk to him/her and the parents on an individual basis. It was always amazing to see that many years after passing out from the school, when students would visit the school just to meet the teachers, Meena Teacher (as she is fondly known to all) would recall every student's name and his/her special memories. The entire teaching staff also nurtured it as a core value and the children who had had the privilege of attending the preschool, cherished the schooling under the leadership of Meena Teacher.

Men leadership characteristics

- **Transactional style**

  Studies indicate that men are more likely to follow the transactional leadership style. Transactional management is a part of leadership that focuses on supervision, organisation, or performance. Closely linking awards and punishments is embedded into transactional management. Such leaders therefore also establish clear, measurable goals and targets and expect the team members to work towards achieving them.

- **Hierarchical structure**

  A hierarchical structure offers better clarity of an individual's roles and responsibilities. Commensurate with transactional leadership focus, hierarchical structure supports close control over goals and targets. It also helps in monitoring individual performance to attribute success and failure. Men leaders therefore may have a preference for such structures and organisational set ups.

- **Focus on performance**

  Leaders expect individuals to do their best in their defined roles. This has a positive impact on business growth and performance. In turn such high performers get great opportunities to rise in the organisations or enhance their roles. On the other hand, such individual excellence should be deployed across other levels for the larger benefit, lest the organisations suffer in the longer run.

- **Direct communication**

  Men leaders often adopt a style of directly communicating their expectations, instructions, directions, and overall requirements to their juniors. After all, it has also to do with the gender differences in communications. Notwithstanding the stereotypes, it can be easily seen that women use non-verbal communication (in simple words, body language!) more often and more effectively than men. Even in verbal and written communication there could be gender peculiarities. It is an interesting topic and readers are encouraged to study the references indicated at the end of the chapter. One should be mindful of such subtle differences and learn to respect them. Successful leaders do recognise these aspects and modulate their behaviours in workplaces.

- **Creating competitions**

  Men leaders encourage their subordinates to compete with each other in order to develop their individual potential. Healthy competition between teams, groups, departments, or individuals leads to progress and is certainly beneficial for the organisation. The flip side of a competitive environment is that those top performers develop tendencies of clinging on to their expertise and as a result, knowledge sharing across the organisation gets restricted. It also leads to the creation of a stressed environment at the workplace.

These prominent ones and many other differences in the leadership styles of men and women truly make them unique. Their effectiveness lies in understanding and addressing the responses of their teams to their own leadership. One must be mindful that despite these trends, one should not conclude that women or men specifically follow such specific styles only. Women leaders quickly learn how poorly people respond to "bossy" behaviours and can cleverly soften their approaches. Also, men leaders, when handling mixed teams change their styles to suit their own teams for more effective leadership.

Some interesting results emerged from the survey carried out by the author to assess the possible bias as seen by the leaders when working and handling subordinates of the opposite gender. In response to the question "To what extent are you comfortable in handling your reportees/colleagues of the opposite gender?", 94% of responders showed a very high degree of comfort (8 on the scale of 1 to 10). On the other side, they also indicated that they were required to modulate their behaviours to overcome some discomfort. As a next response, they indicated the possible reasons for such discomfort as per the following chart.

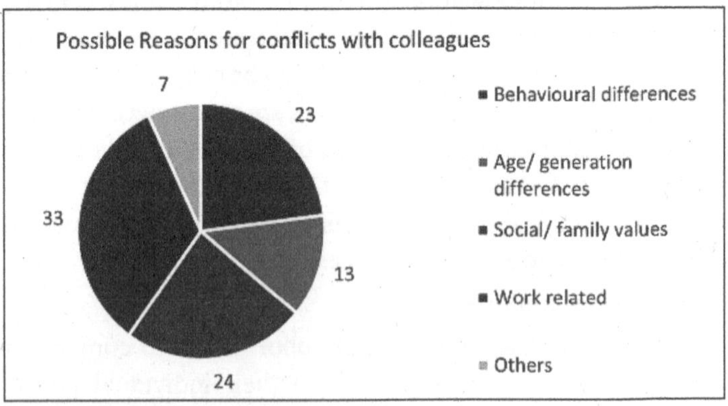

Graph 1 - Survey response: Ease of working with colleagues

Work-related differences, which contributed to 33% was a single most reason, followed by behavioural, social, and age-related perceptions. All these aspects can be overcome with inclusivity policies, orientation, and training to all the teams. Good leaders indeed pay attention to these important facts and overcome the differences quite spectacularly.

As managers

The career journey of women typically might get broken at the level of middle management. For the reasons explained earlier in Chapter 2 (Career Development), women often may be required to take a career break. A significant number of them are unable to start at all or find it difficult to start with full vigour after the break. As a result, the statistics at the middle management level show quite discouraging numbers for gender diversity. With the management studies more focused on men, the changing trend indicates that a good amount of self-assessment and self-help tools are available for young budding managers, both, men, and women.

Given the inclusivity, one must be mindful that women managers differ from men managers in their styles, not skills! As discussed above, there are bound to be personality differences. At the leadership levels, perhaps these differences are offset with grooming, developing maturity, and widening horizons. At the management/middle management level, such behavioural differences do manifest in distinctive management styles or patterns.

- Female managers are said to have higher levels of empathy on one hand and authority on the other hand. Such managers show greater understanding and an ability to appreciate the perspectives of other members but still maintain a higher level of authority.

"Health-Point" polyclinic, is co-owned and managed by Manisha. In her polyclinic, consultancy spaces are rented by about 15 young doctors including Dr Mrunal, my dentist daughter-in-law. Manisha and her trained staff ensure that all administrative requirements are met efficiently so that the doctors can focus on their medical practices. During the day's work, she has a close rapport with all the doctors, and she manages well their otherwise difficult schedules, customer bases and such. But when it comes to her authority as the manager/administrator, she does manage the transition quite effortlessly!

- Women have low levels of social confidence and assertiveness as compared to men. Assertiveness is often expected to be associated with authority. Display of authority is a personal trait and different shades of it can be seen in individual behaviours.

  My memory goes back to 30 years ago, when we were carrying out the installation and commissioning of the state-of-the-art Fatigue testing equipment. The team was led by the manufacturers' representative, a tall, hefty lady. She was a Hydraulics engineer of German origin, and we all were working under her guidance. She would normally not interfere or assert herself when it came to daily work allocations and execution. Some male colleagues therefore started taking her casually. She was a perfectionist, a hardcore trained commissioning expert and would show her authority and assert herself when the menfolk bypassed work safety or lacked a step-by-step approach.
- Female managers show a lower zeal or hunger for power for the sake of it as compared to men. They are more seen to lead with their conscience, focus on providing support and treat their colleagues/fellow team members fairly. In fact, the perception of power itself is different for men and women. Men managers may define the power in the organisation as their ability to utilise resources. They would like to ask for more funds for expansion, aspire to establish and lead new units, etc. Females may interpret power as the freedom to collaborate and transform! They would certainly look for business growth but in a more controlled and transformational manner than an aggressive one.
- Women tend to be more creative and open-minded at work. This has a direct link with their higher level of empathy. Further, they appear to be more methodical and dutiful in their approaches.

Bhagyashri Bhagwat is the Founder and Managing Director, ChemTech Laboratories. What got established in the early '90s as a simple Oil and Chemical analysis laboratory has now expanded its horizon to partner with industries to solve complex product development problems. Bhagyashri deeply empathises with her team as well as customers and has created a vibrant analytical research environment for them. Deeply guided by her core values, technical expertise, and systematic resource creation, she has built a strong and sustaining business. During the recent COVID-19 pandemic, like every industry sector, ChemTech was deeply affected by the lockdown, lack of business and health threats. While most industries of that size had already laid off their staff, Bhagyashri empathised with her team members and decided to bear the loss at least partially. With the human resource intact, post-COVID recovery is seen to be less difficult for the laboratory under her empathetic and dutiful management approach.

Coming to some of the positive traits shown by male managers:

- Men show higher level of confidence and security in their domain. Men try out the application of their knowledge with much more ease when it comes to new work assignments. Industrial psychology indicates that they are more open to taking risks at work.
- While arriving at decisions, men often apply practical and professional knowledge. The practicality is more oriented towards business goals and organisational benefits than individual team members. This greatly enhances their decision-making ability.

  As the saying goes, "Men change world while women improve it!"

As teams

An interesting study report is available with Harvard Business Review. It is titled "In collaborative work cultures women carry more of the weight". The research team has closely examined the behaviour of female and male members of organisational teams.

The base of how strongly the collaborations in teams work is how much value do the members place on relationships. Normally relationship-heavy cultures are characterised by inclusion, personal connection and relationship-based decision making. Relationship-based teams often involve a large number of members, tight time frames and multiple projects. These situations create a collaborative overload. The study outcome indicates that while every member of such teams felt the overload, women members felt the burden disproportionately high.

According to the study, possible reasons could be:

- First, women are more likely to care for the collective, which means they are more likely to step in when they see a gap or ambiguity. There is an important difference in the way men and women view collaboration. Women are more likely to believe "Being a good team player means helping all of my colleagues with what they need to get done." In contrast, men are more likely to believe "Being a good team player is knowing your position and playing it well." In organisations that get work done through informal project teams or that have overlapping accountabilities, this difference in perspective has deep implications on the way men and women engage in collaboration and work in teams.
- Second, women are less likely to carve out time during the workday to focus on their top priorities, because they feel guilty or selfish for doing so. If women do carve out time, they tend to give it away if someone needs them. In organisations, the consequence is that women often end up overscheduled, rushing from meeting to meeting or juggling between different tasks. This can have negative consequences on their careers because they risk appearing scattered, late, and unprepared. Their contributions might go unnoticed if their efforts are fragmented across multiple efforts. They will not have time for focused work. On the other hand, men are more likely to carry out distraction-free work for a longer time on multiple occasions.

Women at the management level were found to experience far greater burnout and frustration than men. Yet they were also more likely to invest their time to establish work practices that would benefit others. Women not only take on more than their share of the collaborative load, but they are also more likely to take action to reduce the overall workload in their team or department.

In the early part of my career, I often struggled with my urge to step out of my role and help others. While it was a very welcome gesture for my colleagues, I would get overworked and end up missing my own project deadlines. My Head of Department, in my annual appraisal brought this up and candidly told me that I should learn to say "No"! The personal characteristic which I assumed to be having a positive impact, in a competitive and male-dominated environment needed some modulation! I was initially surprised at that feedback but accepted it with an open mind and worked in the next few years to change it. I owe a great deal of my professional development to my former HoD, who inculcated in me very high technical abilities, work ethics and many more professional qualities. But all said and done, even today, my instinct (at work or in personal life), is to step out and help others!

In conclusion, the differences in management and leadership styles or peculiarities of men and women have a great impact on the work culture. The organisations or team leaders should keenly examine the team composition, neutralise and balance out such factors and develop a culture of mutual accountability. Mutuality with the combination of clear understanding, accountability and transparency are the key aspects of success for gender-balanced teams.

Fig. 3 - Diversity and inclusion in teams (Illustration from Pixabay)

"Baja" is an iconic student competition organised every year by Society for Automotive Engineers (SAE). In this pan-India event, engineering teams from all colleges participate enthusiastically. It involves designing your racing vehicles, competing in design, validation, and finally actual racing on the dirt track! The actual event runs for a few days and sees a great deal of adrenaline rush! More so, it involves months of relentless work by competing teams. As a part of SAE leadership, I love to keenly observe the individual students' skills, their team dynamics, and overall competitive performances. Depending on the college demography, some teams are all boys, all girls and many times, mixed ones. Some teams excel in specific technical criteria and stand out with their individual skills. But it is my observation that the overall championship title is every time lifted by a well-balanced team, which also happens to be gender-balanced.

Traditional and non-traditional careers

For a long time, teaching and education were considered to be the best and most suited careers for women. Other similar careers being cabin service and hospitality, healthcare and nursing, entertainment industry, event management and branding, law, fashion designing, body care/ cosmetics, sales and marketing, journalism and public relations, banking and insurance, human relations, government jobs and such.

Similarly, many jobs are traditionally seen as men's jobs. Some such examples are plumbing and machine maintenance, defence services, automotive and heavy machinery, goods transportation, corporate leadership positions, financial leadership, stand-up comedy, aviation and shipping industry, construction and mining and many such.

With the changing times, men and women are increasingly moving into and are succeeding in non-traditional careers. Their stories are highly motivating for others to follow in their footsteps. In fact, there are many untapped careers, which remain non-traditional for women as well as men.

The biggest advantage of choosing a non-traditional career is being able to follow your dreams and self-satisfaction. It also offers a great opportunity to learn new skills, new subjects and knowledge and it invariably comes with higher monetary rewards. There are of course several disadvantages and a higher level of struggle in achieving progress in such unconventional choices.

Behavioural stereotypes for men and women

Gender stereotypes are both descriptive and prescriptive in nature. Descriptive components are those perceptions about what men and women typically do whereas prescriptive components are about what men and women should do or are anticipated to do. It is interesting to note that both these components undergo change with age, experience, and overall exposure to gender-inclusive societies.

Further, by the very nature of prescriptive stereotypes, it indicates approved (or disapproved) behaviours. Violations of such prescriptions therefore create strong reactions such as disappointment, anger, moral outrage, etc. whereas violations of descriptive stereotypes result in surprise, amusement, and such.

Just to give examples, women are expected and prescribed to be communicative and avoid dominance. In case there is a violation of this perception, and a woman appears to be dominant, she is disliked. In another example, the descriptive stereotype of men is that they are emotionally strong and avoid showing their emotions. If a man, watching the latest movie starts sobbing when a highly emotional drama sequence happens, everyone looks at him in amazement.

I recently studied a research paper that states that in fact, adult men are viewed more negatively for the violation of stereotypes than women are viewed for their violations! Even a single "unmanly" or "feminine" act would discount the man's status! One can therefore imagine what pressure it must create at the workplace for men to avoid showing weakness. In fact, men would be judged more harshly for "feminine" behaviour than women for "masculine" behaviour!

I would like to cite here my own experience. My upward progress in the corporate world was quite spectacular. In the otherwise male-dominated automotive sector, my emergence initially at organisational, then national level and later international level expert was incredibly significant. It was purely on account of my acquiring specialised skills in automotive technologies related to vehicular safety, emissions, green fuels, electric mobility and many more. People around me know me as a soft-spoken, unassuming lady having iron nerves! During an important meeting in the Ministry, Additional Secretary, Government of India mentioned appreciatively that I have a lot of masculine traits when it comes to strongly handling the otherwise difficult automotive industry! Ignoring its gender bias, I conveniently took it as a compliment!

Appraisals and performance reviews

Traditionally, organisations follow set formats for employee appraisals. These formats are usually designed keeping men in mind. There is a need to re-examine and suitably modify such formats to address gender neutrality. Subjective as well as objective assessment is often based on personalities rather than specific roles. As a result, women are more likely to receive negative or more critical assessment feedback than their male colleagues.

Fig. 4 - Gender bias in performance appraisals (Artist- Durga Tilak)

Further, managers are humans and not machines. Their appraisals are based on their personalities, biases, and stereotypes. Managers perceive women to possess different traits than men. For example, women are expected to have better team-based skills while men are expected to be more independent. Such assumptions and behavioural stereotypes as discussed in the earlier paragraphs might result in men and women being put through different assessment lenses.

These are often the outcome of subconscious and implicit biases. We normally also have a tendency of perceiving others' personalities based on our own personality. It therefore becomes essential that gender biases are eliminated from the assessment process and it is made as objective and fact-based as possible by avoiding judgemental and subjective/descriptive behavioural reviews.

Another interesting observation is that similar behaviour by men and women can be described entirely differently. For example, behaviour that is regarded as "confident" or "assertive" in the case of a man could be defined as "abrasive" in the case of a woman. When women are assertive and display leadership, they are often described using phrases like "bossy", "aggressive", "pushy", etc. As discussed earlier, there is a generalised perception that women are supportive and helpful to the members and colleagues, their accomplishments are perceived to be the result of teamwork rather than individual performance or excellence, unlike those of the male colleagues.

Another difference is that the evaluation for men is based more on their technical expertise and key results. On the other hand, evaluation for women is based on their soft skills. Critical feedbacks often include suggestions for men to develop their skills, while women on the other hand receive more negative feedback/criticism but not specific, constructive suggestions for personal development.

Stereotypes in recruitments

Women experience biases during the hiring process also. Hiring team members make assumptions about parental responsibilities. Even though men also have family obligations outside of work, women overwhelmingly face speculations about their ability to accomplish work commitments with their family responsibilities on hand. Women are always questioned about their leadership abilities and this presumption might prevent them from getting hired for management positions. There are still some stereotypes that certain jobs or positions are more suited for either men or women. It hinders the role fit at the time of hiring.

Using standardised selection tools (such as structured interviews and job knowledge tests) and procedures which are resistant to bias enables the hiring teams to minimise the possibilities of gender biases while selecting the right candidate for the announced and stated requirements. Even hiding the gender-related information helps in the initial screening. Hiring by the committee is also a good practice. The team decisions tend to be more resistant to biases than individual decisions.

Entrepreneurship stereotypes

Think entrepreneur, think man, is the stereotype so deeply settled in and around our society. So much so that we seem to neglect our statistics. About 15 million small and medium enterprises are women-owned or controlled. In terms of proportions, it works out to be 20% percentile of the entrepreneurship index. Another paradigm is it is the younger people who are more capable of solving significant business challenges and take up entrepreneurship at an early phase of their lives. In reality, if you see opportunities and find creative ways to come out with solutions, you are the entrepreneur, regardless of how old you are or what your background may be.

The traits associated with entrepreneurship include self-esteem, risk-taking ability, autonomous decision-making, confidence, ability to control, resilience and such. Putting all these together, we arrive at a male entrepreneur!

The female entrepreneurship studies clearly indicate that successful females also demonstrate very similar characteristics and they use these traits to maximise their business opportunities in the same way the men would do. Sheryl Sandberg, COO, Meta Facebook, amply makes it clear how women can frame and embrace risk.

Fig. 5 - Women in entrepreneurship (Artist- Durga Tilak)

Research Reports in India on women entrepreneurship identify some major hurdles that women face in the growth and success of their enterprises. The access to finances through formal banking or other funding agencies or for that matter informal money lenders is one of the major stumbling blocks for women. Even access to formal and informal business networks becomes restrictive to women having an adverse impact on their growth and potential.

Clear facts

When it comes to numbers, India has more women-owned enterprises than many other countries. A closer look however reveals interesting facts.

- Women-owned enterprises are growing. Over the past decade, women-owned enterprises have increased from 14% to 20%, as per government sources. This is with the help of national and state governments, investors, banks, financial and educational institutions, and, most of all, the enterprising female workforce.
- India still faces a large gap compared with peers in developed markets such as the US and UK, and developing markets such as Brazil, Russia, and Nigeria.
- Women-owned enterprises in India are largely single-person enterprises. This leads to lower returns and employment.
- True entrepreneurship among women is overrepresented in numbers. In many cases, they are owned, but not controlled or run by women. Women are "on paper" shown as entrepreneurs.

There are thankfully quite a few inspiring success stories like Mallika Srinivasan (TAFE), Kiran Majumdar Shaw (Biocon), Ekta Kapoor (Balaji Telefilms), Indra Nooyi (PepsiCo) which would provide the beacon to other aspiring young women.

References:

1. Women in Workplace (2019 Report by McKinsey and Company)

Chapter 7

Challenges for Work-Life Balance

अब तो दिन रात पे हि आके रूकता हैं
मुझे याद हैं .... पेहले एक श्याम भी हुआ करती थी
- गुलझार

What is Work-Life Balance (WLB)

Work-Life Balance is a term used for the idea that one needs time for work- and non-work-related activities. Non-work-related activities would include family, friends, personal development, societal involvement, and such. The saying goes, "All work and no play makes Jack a dull boy". But work, whether paid or voluntary, is also recognised as being important for personal satisfaction, so "all play" will also be no good! This is where the balancing act comes.

The idea that rest is vital for productive work output is quite ancient. "And on 7th day God ended his work, which he made, and he rested on 7th day", says the Bible. Even God needs a break after long hard work!

In the 1800s, during and after the Industrial Revolution, the workers needed a day off. Thus, started the concept of "weekend". In those days, work would be only manual and thus on weekly offs, the workers would be away from their work, physically as well as mentally and they would be able to genuinely rest.

Fig. 1 - Balancing both worlds, the art (Illustration from Pixabay)

The phrase 'Work-Life Balance' is rather recent in origin. It was probably first used in the UK in the late 1970s and later in the USA in the mid-1980s. It has assumed a new dimension and meaning with the recent trends that have made it possible for workers to stay in touch 24 hours a day, 7 days a week. Smartphones, remote working technology, virtual teams, and such mean that even during off-duty hours people find it challenging to stay disconnected and thus are unable to genuinely rest well.

The famous scientist, Albert Einstein once said "Life is like riding a bicycle. To keep our balance, we must keep moving". Move, we must, but in which direction? In pursuit of what? All those activities, whether obligatory or voluntary that we undertake, fill up our time scale so very quickly that we hardly realise that we need to balance them out in order to make our lives happy and tranquil.

Interference: Life to Work and Work to Life (LWI and WLI)

Every adult human (men and women alike) plays multiple roles in life. Life itself has two major parts, personal and professional. In each part also there are multiple, conflicting, overlapping and sometimes even fuzzy roles. Employer, employee, boss, team member, mentor, mentee, leader, follower, entrepreneur, and many such roles keep changing in professional life. On the other hand, personal level roles are much more complex, son/daughter, father/mother, sibling, friend, caregiver, bread-earner, home manager, educator, extended family member, and many more.

Each of these roles comes with a baggage of expectations, commitments, and obligations. During every phase of life, the roles keep on changing, toggling, and enhancing. There is a large interference amongst different roles in personal life itself.

Similar is the case in professional life also. The complexity further increases when there is an interference of professional life in personal life (WLI). The same is true for reverse flow as well, resulting in interference of personal life in professional life (LWI).

It is a matter of research to establish whether such interferences are more in the case of women than men. Under all circumstances, it is a fact that it starts affecting the health, wellbeing, relationship, and resource management of professionals. There arises the need to address the issues and restore the balance, which in other words is Work-Life Balance.

Maslow's hierarchy of needs

Wide research has been done so far to examine whether Maslow's famous pyramid depicting the hierarchy of needs has any correlation with the work-life balance. There are mixed conclusions about it. However, the subject is quite interesting and worth discussing here.

Fig. 2 - Hierarchy of needs

According to Maslow, people have needs and they are to be met in the order of hierarchy. The needs can be visualised in the form of a pyramid, the basic needs (such as food, shelter) occupying the base of the pyramid indicating higher priority (Fig. 2). Then people want to feel safe, then be loved and belong to a group. Further, they move to self-esteem, cognitive needs, aesthetic needs, and such. At the top of the pyramid is self-actualisation or achieving one's full potential.

What can be interpreted in reality is that work provides for basic needs: money earned provides food, and shelter and a regular income means safety. The lower levels are all largely met through aspects of working. Work also allows people to belong to a group and doing well at work boosts self-esteem. At the top of the pyramid, however, are needs which are hard to meet with work alone, and this is where lifestyle choices, and having time for leisure become important.

On the other hand, the interpretation is flawed according to some other analysts and researchers. These ideas were postulated much earlier and that too in the context of motivation and not intended at analysis of life. Human needs change dynamically and hence require constant attention. We get hungry every few hours and get sleepy at the end of the day. Thus, movement across the levels of needs is not unidirectional and hierarchal but runs through the levels of satisfaction as and when there is a depletion of that particular level.

To maintain total well-being, you need to constantly prioritise and re-prioritise what requires attention. Thus, when we realise that the needs are dynamic, life becomes more interesting than the "I havc too many things to do" feeling. You can gain control over what you can choose to do.

Effects of good WLB

A good balance has numerous positive effects, including less stress, low burnout, more productivity, and a better sense of wellbeing. This not only benefits the individuals but also the organisations. In fact, the employers who are committed to providing an environment that supports better WLB, are likely to save cost, have less absenteeism and enjoy a more loyal and productive workforce.

Global scenario

In August 2015, the European Commission published a Roadmap for the initiative "A new start to address the challenges of work-life balance faced by working families", which will replace the 2008 Commission's proposal to amend the Maternity Leave Directive. The objective of this new initiative is to modernise and adapt the current European Union (EU) legal and policy framework to allow parents with children and/or those with dependent relatives to better balance caring and professional responsibilities, encourage a more equitable use of work-life balance policies between women and men, and strengthen gender equality in the labour market.

In its 2016 Work Programme, the European Commission has also announced a 'new start' initiative on work-life balance covering both legislative and non-legislative measures. The intention is to review the EU regulatory and policy landscape in this field with a view to better tackling the challenges of work-life balance for parents and people with caring responsibilities. The review of the current situation indicates that the countries in EU are at quite different levels of measures.

On the other hand, the impact of family and WLB policies of corporates on their business performance is also of great interest to these countries. Survey reports indicate a correlation between the two. Analysis was carried out for some listed companies and findings support the idea that introducing work-life balance practices benefits the company with respect to talent retention and higher employee engagement. It also was concluded that these policies had a positive impact on productivity, cost control and business results.

There are counterarguments that an increase in cost offsets the quantitative benefits. It is however uniformly agreed that WLB policies contribute to increasing employee satisfaction.

Indian studies: Impact of age, gender, experience (demographics) on WLB

The scenario in India at non-legislative measures follows a similar trend. Many of the research reports are available. Some studies at the national level are carried out to examine the impact of age, gender, work experience etc. on the perceptions related to WLB. Some interesting ones are highlighted below.

In the service sector, the Bank of Baroda for their employees in Gujarat carried out a survey to examine if the age of employees has any significant impact on the WLB assessment. Accordingly, they surveyed employees in the age ranges 20-25, 25-35, 35-55 and beyond 55 years. Some significant findings were, WLB was significantly low in the age group 35 to 55. Persons in this age group often have multiple challenges in personal life as well as at work. Another significant observation was that men appeared to be less satisfied with their WLB than their female colleagues, having similar work profiles. Further, employees having work experience of more than 7 years, were less satisfied than those who were relatively new in their careers.

Another report on Bengaluru city involved the perception of women employees working in diverse sectors like IT, BPO, Marketing, Insurance, Banking and Education. Although it is a relatively old survey (the year 2010-11), the findings are quite valid to date. Men and women having similar work profiles were participants of the survey.

Based on the analysis, it is concluded that there is a significant relationship between demographic variables and the work-life balance of women employees. Such findings will be an important input in designing appropriate policies for employees to address work-life balance issues. Work-life balance initiatives designed to help employees balance their work and personal lives are not only an option but also a necessity for many employers today.

In a separate survey carried out as a research project for this book, the response to the question "Do you sometimes experience that your professional life is interfering with personal life? To what extent?" is as under:

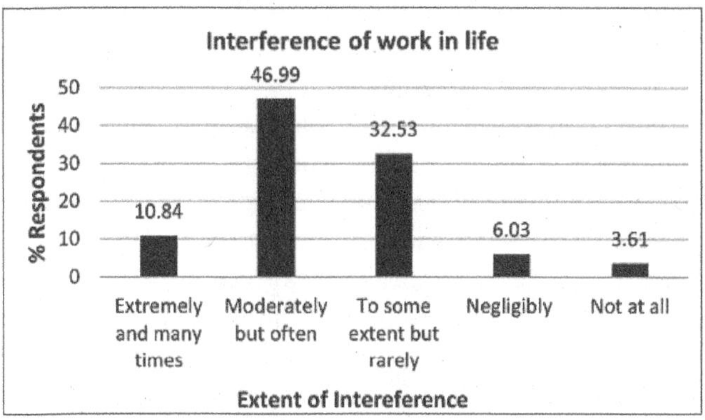

Graph 1 - Survey Result: Interference of Work on Life

As seen in Graph 1 above, about 57% of respondents expressed that this interference is moderate but often or extreme and many times!

Impact of better WLB at 3 levels

At the individual level, the WLB means the ability to join or combine work with other dimensions of human life: home, family, health, social activity, private interests, etc. From this perspective, WLB provides psychological well-being, high self-esteem, satisfaction, and an overall sense of harmony in life. Individuals keeping the balance between work and personal life are happier, healthier, and more creative. It is said by scholars that only successful persons dealing with three areas of life at the same time (in the family, in the workplace and in local communities) provide an individual with appropriate development and psychological balance. It should be emphasised at this point, however, that the equilibrium point is not the same for everyone, and the reconciliation of professional and non-professional life is made possible by the appropriate organisation of time and support from family and colleagues.

At the level of organisation, the work-life balance means appropriate management system and personnel policy conducive to maintaining the balance by the employees. It is also the organisation's use of solutions aimed at improving the quality of work and life. From the point of view of the organisation, the employees' WLB means more opportunities for its development, also through an increase in productivity and innovation.

In the broadest sense, at the level of society, the realisation of the idea of WLB means such an organisation of the labour market that improves the ease of finding work and increases the sense of security of employment. The development of WLB at the society level may be associated with the introduction of specific formal solutions by the state and its agencies (within the broader labour market policies or the so-called 'pro-family policy') or based on the initiatives undertaken by the institutions forming the labour market (including the entrepreneurs themselves), resulting from the managers' high awareness of work-life-balance.

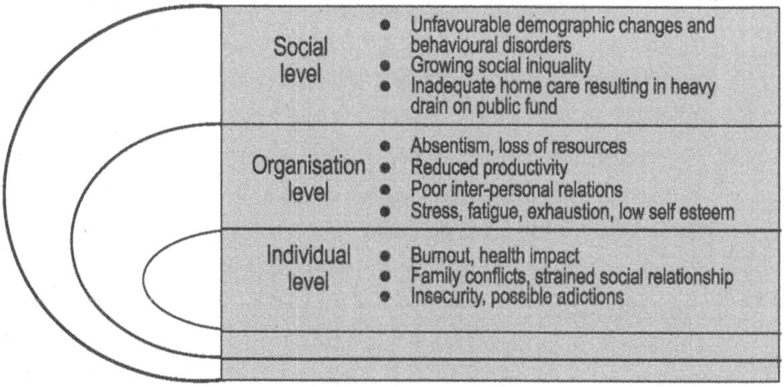

Fig. 3 - Impact of better WLB

Some good policies

The instruments most offered by employers to help employees maintain work-life balance include:

- More flexible forms of work and working time organisation, as well as some non-standard forms of employment (outsourcing and contracting work, temporary work, task-based working time, on-call work, equivalent working time, substitution, or job-sharing)
- Various types of leaves and allowances and exemptions from obligations of work, provided to the employee because of their need to fulfil family responsibilities
- Benefits realised in various forms by the employer for employees who use alternative forms of care for dependents (for e.g., a company kindergarten/creche, day nursery facilities) either free or subsidised in proximity
- Bonuses (financial and non-financial) to the employees who are forced to reconcile work and caring responsibilities, help with childcare costs: Information and financial support to meet childcare costs, either in cash or reimbursement.
- Assistance for elderly care: Offering information on centres for elderly care and facilitating engaging such services
- Information about schools: Providing the employee with information on schools, their ratings and sometimes facilitating children admissions

- Job sharing positions: Two people can share a full-time job in the company. Such an arrangement works quite well for their mutual benefit and increases the cost-effectiveness of human resource utilisation
- Extension of permissions: The company establishes a maternity or paternity leave beyond the minimum legal period on a case-to-case basis
- Flexible working hours: Employees can decide at what time they start their working hours and what time they leave the company, although total duty hours must be completed.
- Part-time work: Employees work part-time.
- Compressed work schedule: Employees can work longer hours and receive in return a day or half a day off a week. This is a quite common practice in the industry where workers get compensatory off in lieu of the additional work they have already put in
- Telecommuting job: Employees may develop their work through an internet connection from home or any place that is most comfortable for them.
- Leisure activities: The company introduces leisure and cultural programmes for employees and their families. Within this policy, discounts are also offered by the company for activities with the same purpose (such as membership in recreational clubs or social circles)
- Medical check-up: Employees and in some cases their family members have health checks done by the organisation.
- Advisory services and professional support: Legal, financial, tax, psychological, family or career advice.

Balancing act

All said and done, WLB is not an entitlement of benefit due from your employer! You must create it. In the context of WLB, it is often misunderstood that the balance must be between the two aspects, work in one pan of the balance and personal life in another. In fact, balancing has a wider connotation. During any running day, we have a series of activities to be done and we balance out our time depending on the importance and priority.

A person is much more than what s/he is seen in professional life. S/he has a persona, family, society, friends and much more. All these roles demand attention and one would juggle one's time and priority accordingly. While giving her best to professional life or the job, from where does she get time and energy for the rest of her priorities?

Work-life balance is not just dividing the hours in a day evenly between work and life. It is more about having the flexibility to getting things done in your professional life while still having time and energy to do things that you want in your personal life. There may still be days in the week, where you work longer than normal duty hours but then you will also have time on other days for personal activities.

Here are a few important things to remember for getting better WLB.

- **There is no perfect WLB**

  There could be days where your job or career demands more from you and on other occasions, you could easily take a vacation, take your partner on a romantic date and on still other occasions, be with your ailing parents.

  Life is quite dynamic and each phase, in fact, each day of personal life is also quite unique. So also, at work, the requirements keep changing. New bosses, changing deadlines, sudden changes in priorities, technological advancements, changing behaviours and many more. With great efforts, what balances out today may completely go out of balance tomorrow.

- **Finding the job that you love**

  One is not expected to love every activity and aspect at work. There are several activities that we detest doing or they do not fit into the defined role or are even outside of our capability. But as a whole, the work should offer excitement and joy. If we start getting work-related nightmares or start hating the work, there is something wrong and it is perhaps time to look for another job.

  Most of our productive time goes at work. Making it satisfying is therefore particularly important for being happy. This happiness helps greatly in creating better WLB.

- **Superwoman syndrome**

  Men and women are required to play multiple roles in personal and professional lives. Parenthood, caregiver, loving partner, friend, associate, colleague, boss and many more. These roles keep alternating and changing with time. With the prevalent social norms, it is the woman who becomes a target of expectations. These expectations come in early life from siblings, parents and later from growing children, ailing or ageing parents and in-laws, husband, extended family, neighbours, and friends. On top of everything, expectations from colleagues, bosses and many more at the workplace keep piling. The expectations are sometimes stated but many times remain unstated. A woman is thus surrounded by overwhelming tide waves that pull and push her in a random manner. Her expectations about herself add to another level of complexity.

  Women often want to do everything and want to do it well! They in fact want to do it best! This situation often leads to something well-known, the Superwoman syndrome. In achieving all that is in their mind, women often forget about self-care!

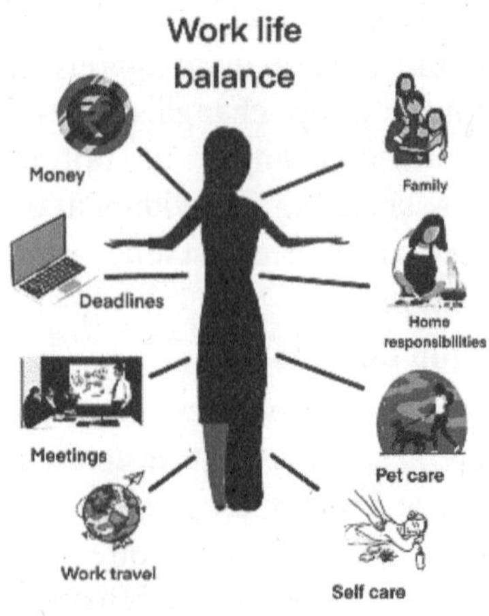

Fig. 4 - "Superwoman Syndrome" (Artist- Durga Tilak)

Self-care and prioritising yourself

Remember your air-travels? You are reminded that in case of emergency, you must wear your oxygen mask first before you help your child to do so! Self-care is therefore like an oxygen mask. A woman may be super-strong, powerful, and most independent and thinks that she can carry the whole world on her shoulders. But not without her oxygen!

Your overall physical, emotional, and mental wellbeing is very critical, and it does not come automatically. The deeper we get engaged in our professional lives, the more we tend to neglect ourselves. In fact, work anxiety, depression, undue stress, long duty hours and many more such factors take their toll on health. It further reduces the efficiency and diminishes joy from work creating an imbalance.

Here are a few small things you can implement in daily routine. It would help in overcoming the superwoman syndrome and get yourself your own oxygen!

- Make your happiness list
- Small things like having your first cup of tea on the terrace, listening to your favourite song, holding a kitten in hand are often very valuable. The list can include many more small ones and even big ones like getting a vacation in the deep forest!
- Use your list to bring in happiness
- We must find ways to get the list. All it needs is often a concerted effort and prioritisation to achieve most of it. The happiness starts trickling down first and then pouring in!
- Create a support system

  Availability of domestic help is a big positive factor in Indian urban and semi-urban areas. On many occasions, support from parents or in-laws may also be available when requested. In the case of nuclear families, the large friend circle also offers a great deal of support and a helping hand. Creating a reliable, faithful, and committed support system by blending such possible options is the need of the hour. It takes personal efforts and skills to sustain such a support system and nurture it for mutual benefit.
- Asking for help does not make one weak. On the other hand, it shows magnanimity in seeking help and reciprocating when needed.

I am reminded of the most difficult phase of my career. I had a very demanding job and my commitment to my work involved extensive domestic/international travels and long, stressful duty hours. This was also the time when both my parents were ailing and bedridden for long stretches. Apart from managing my own household, old mother-in-law, teenage son, husband's business support, etc. I was also managing my parent's household and their own domiciliary hospitalisation. At one time, I had created a support system of record 7 servants! 2 women for round-the-clock nursing care for mother, 2 men for father, 1 cleaning maid, 1 cooking maid and 1 driver-turned-general attendant! I would visit my parents every evening, oversee arrangements, review medical progress and such. Parents would utter their frustration, anger, and displeasure while the staff would put forth their complaints against each other, against my parents, in general, against what they thought was not going their own way!

I would patiently deal with them on most occasions. One time, I decided to apply my management technique. I called for a meeting of all 7 of the servants in front of my parents. I explained to them that it was true that the oldies were not in the best of humour and getting difficult day by day. But it was also true that all the group, including me, existed there because of them. We better do our jobs properly and with affection, I said! After that extraordinary meeting, the team did remarkably better!

- **Learning to say no**

  Many of us struggle to say no when we actually want to say no! Since childhood, we are taught to please others and saying yes to please others is one facet of this upbringing. In our busy lives and tight schedules, we are often required to address other people's requests. That is where it helps in deciding whether we actually wish to honour the request. If we do not want, it is most appropriate to say so and remove the guilt from our mind than hating to do what we are forced to do because we could not say no!

  The famed psychologist, Bill Crawford said one time, "One key to successful relationships is learning to say no without guilt so that you can say yes without resentment."

- **Prioritise your health**

  There is absolutely nothing wrong in getting sanctioned sick leave to get into better shape. Overworking when you are ill will further prevent you from getting better. In fact, prioritising health does not necessarily call for drastic life changes. All it needs is fitting into your daily routine a dedicated time for fitness activity of your choice and ability.

- **Give time to family and friends**

  Spending quality time with family and friends makes a great difference in increasing happiness. With young children, there is a good chance that we will spend a lot of time. The pattern however changes as children grow, spouses get busy in their own way and with all good intentions, finding out common family time becomes challenging.

As we grow older and the life becomes faster, our time allocation for friends diminishes, un-intentionally though! Spending time with friends is often the best and biggest stressbuster and hence it's worth putting friends on a high priority list!

Creating long-lasting bonds with family and friends is the best and most fulfilling experience in my view. It takes effort, but it is worth every bit of it!

- **Time management**

  Time is sometimes seen as the scarcest resource the professionals have at their disposal. Thus, for better WLB, time management becomes quite important. In simple words, time management is the process of planning and exercising conscious control of the time spent on specific activities. Several tools and techniques can be used for increasing effective time management at the personal as well as professional levels. The heart of time management is to remember that nobody is too busy, it is just a matter of priorities!

  Sonali started her career as a junior engineer in Pune. After her wedding, she had to shift to Lonavala and that meant everyday commute to work in Pune, which is 60 km away. Over the last 20 years, she has been successfully juggling personal and professional commitments. She is now a senior executive in her organisation and fully committed to her profession and very happy in her personal life. She has adopted many of the time management techniques to create appropriate spaces for important things in life.

- **Set boundaries and work hours**

  It helps in setting boundaries for yourself as well as co-workers to avoid burnout. It is also important to stick to these boundaries to the extent possible and let others know about your boundaries and schedules.

  In certain professions like medical care, setting clear boundaries may neither be possible nor appropriate. Mrunal, my daughter-in-law is a dentist by profession and in the last 5 years, we all have learnt to adjust with her changing boundaries!

Dealing with personal tragedy

Life throws challenges at us and in some instances, we are hit by personal tragedies. We are taken off guard and likely to lose emotional balance. In crisis situations and in handling personal tragedies, one can learn to gain strength from those great souls who make difference in our lives.

"When we meet real tragedy in life, we can react in two ways - either by losing hope and falling into self-destructive habits, or by using the challenge to find our inner strength. Thanks to the teachings of Buddha, I have been able to take this second way," said the Dalai Lama!

Fig. 5 - Handling personal tragedies

I am also reminded of Sindhutai Sapkal, the noted social worker and activist. She was conferred with Doctorate in Literature by the D Y Patil Institute of Technology and Research. She was the recipient of several awards and accolades and the list is topped by the highest civilian award, Nari Shakti Puraskar. Sindhutai was lovingly called Mai (mother) because she was a mother to numerous orphans, neglected ones and destitute women.

Sindhutai was born in a cattle-grazing family and being an unwanted child, she was referred to as Chindhi, meaning a torn piece of cloth or a rag. Like many other girl children, she had a troubled childhood and an early marriage to a much elderly husband. In her new home, she fought against the exploitation of peasant women. At the age of 20, in an advanced stage of pregnancy, she was beaten and thrown out of the house by her husband to let her die.

But die, she did not! In half-dead condition, she gave birth to a girl child. The girl was named Mamata (meaning compassion) and Sindhutai struggled to live by begging, rag picking and sheltering herself and Mamata in cemeteries. She chose to stay at cemeteries to protect herself from the prowling men! She later recalled that she found herself safer in the company of dead bodies than surrounded by the living villains! She somehow overcame the urge to commit suicide and realised that there were several orphans and needy women like her. She decided to continue living for them and thus become a mother to all such children. Sindhutai, the selfless soul at one time donated her biological daughter to a charitable trust, only to eliminate the possible feeling of partiality between her daughter and adopted children. She used all the award money to build orphanages in Pune district. More than 300 children are now living in these orphanages.

Sindhutai Sapkal, caring mother for orphans

Another committed person I have closely known was Late Shri Chandmal Parmar, Chairman Late Kum Rajashree Parmar Memorial Foundation. Chandmalji and the Foundation received several national awards for their contributions to Road Safety. His work in this area started because of the unfortunate death of his young daughter, Rajashree in a tragic road accident. The personal tragedy turned him into a crusader for road safety. He also fought for establishing the Good Samaritan policy that would save lives in the golden hours of the accident; onlookers often withdraw from the accident scene fearing police harassment.

Be a good manager

As a manager, you would be partly involved in creating balance (or imbalance!) for your team members. Some thoughts here will help in being a good manager for a team that is struggling hard to create their own balances.

- Know what your members are striving for- Everyone has different needs. It is also a fact that not everyone clearly understands or can communicate their needs to the manager. It therefore helps to develop dialogue, talking to team members and understanding them. Organisational rules are often impersonal and may not address individual requirements. Within the managerial authority, it helps to be flexible to address specific requirements such as flexible timing, temporary change of role, sharing responsibility, etc.
- Set a good example- The team looks up to the manager and follows the lead. If you keep on sending emails and placing calls to your subordinates even after work hours, they will conclude that it is the norm and that is expected from them too.
- Conveying to employees what their options are is a good practice. Employers have a formal system of such communication at the time of employment but that is not adequate. People often overlook such details at joining times and it helps if the manager himself conveys to current employees. Also, I have seen some managers having a private talk with the parent-to-be employee and have clarity on the

work and personal commitments of the individual. Such dialogues are indeed very reassuring and help in building strong bonds.

- Stay at the forefront- WLB trends are changing, and they are changing really fast! For being competitive in the job market, corporates are evolving better and more relevant facilities. Managers should keep fresh offerings in mind while managing the teams.

At work, asking for and granting someone a leave of absence sometimes becomes an ordeal. Managers are often stingy when it comes to permitting team members to be absent from busy work schedules whatsoever may be the reasons for absence.

I am reminded of an interesting incident about 30 years ago. Our dog, Cherry, was expected to deliver pups for the first time. I was perhaps more anxious than she was, and I was not at all clear about how to do the midwife role if need be! My other worry was, if she delivers during the daytime when I am away on work, then what? One morning when I was about to step out for work, she looked at me with an appeal in her eyes and I decided to stay back. Soon it became evident that the delivery time was nearing. I called my boss and requested a day off. It was rather unusual for me to be absent in an unplanned manner and he therefore asked what the matter was. I gave the real reason, and he immediately sanctioned my leave. After quite a dramatic birth of total of 6 pups, things were under control and the next day I went to work. Boss called me and laughed aloud and said that he had heard the weirdest reason for asking for a casual leave and I reciprocated saying that it was indeed true and fully justified!

Fig. 6 - Spending time with family (Image from Pixabay)

Another incident way back in 1980! Hemant was a young professional and worked under a boss who was very conventional. Hemant and his close friend Ramesh decided to drive down on their bikes from Pune to Dharwad. Why Dharwad? Because they wanted to witness from there the Total Solar Eclipse, which is quite a rare opportunity. Having arranged the adventure trip (in those days, 400+ km one way on a bike was indeed an adventure) both went to the boss and put up a request for leave for 2 days. On hearing the reason, the boss was speechless. He saw no justification at all in their reason "to see Solar Eclipse" and asked the guys that they should change it to some docile justification such as "urgent personal work", only then he would be able to sanction their leaves!

But then there are other bosses who stay in the forefront and change with times. Hemant was lucky in later years to work under such a dynamic and flexible boss, Vinod. He would encourage his team to do better in balancing their personal lives and work. In fact, he himself would set such examples and Hemant remembers occasions when Vinod would take a day off to watch the India-Pakistan cricket match on TV!

Humour at work

Humour is the best medicine is said and experienced time and again. We Indians tend to be too serious at work! Somehow it does not go well in the work culture to laugh aloud, make fun of each other and still be good and committed employees!

Vehicles are tested and certified by the laboratories/institutes that are authorised by the government. These tests are often quite involved, elaborate and complex. Obviously, there is a very stressed atmosphere in the lab. In the early '80s, there were a handful of vehicle models. Any new model introduction would be an extremely exciting event. Both, testing teams and vehicle manufacturer's teams would keenly carry out their tasks. On one such occasion, the manufacturer had brought a trendsetting 2-wheeler, which later became an iconic Indian scooter.

My colleague Shrikant, the Test Engineer, observed that the scooter had a trendy front and quite imposing lighting/signalling devices. He said in an observant but innocent manner that if the vehicle has a frontal impact, the whole show will be marred. The design team overheard him and took it personally! Perhaps their professional ego was hurt. One of them retorted, if a person falls, and take the example of the test person himself, his face also will be injured or disfigured. Does it therefore mean that such a person should not have good looks?! His remarks later cleared off all the tension!

Realigning for family priorities

WLB is not only specific to those individuals who are engaged in active jobs, working professions or careers. There are several women and occasionally men, who are unable to make their own career because of heavy and undivided priority to family. WLB is equally important for all, especially moms, homemakers, housewives and nowadays, work-from-home moms.

For homemakers, the work never ends, and it therefore becomes particularly challenging to draw a clear line with personal priorities. All the discussion above is equally relevant with the understanding that "professional life" corresponds to "family life" for homemakers.

In the early stages of raising a family and then towards the middle age, family priorities and commitments often overpower the urge to invest time for self-development. Soon these demands diminish and the person, especially ladies, find that they have a lot of time and energy at their disposal. The wise and enthusiastic ones do pick up the threads which were left behind and make their own mark and achieve a new balance in their lives.

Sadhana is a close friend, who dedicated her quality time, energy, and soul to bring up her both children. Sadhana herself was a bright and accomplished person but chose to put her career on hold. Her daughter is a really gifted singer and has been giving live performances since she was barely 5-6 years young. Sadhana focussed on the daughter's development, practice sessions, studies and in addition, special care. The need for special care arose as her daughter developed some clinical problem in one eye. Sadhana's whole focus thus shifted from her own career to the girl's upbringing, development and enabling her to achieve her dreams. Despite all possible medical treatment, the daughter lost sight in one eye at a very tender age. Even the second eye is diagnosed with a similar problem and the treatment continues. After a long struggle, the daughter is now a brilliant young lady, with excellent academic degree in hand and a golden voice that enthrals everybody. She has established herself very successfully in vocal light music live shows. It is indeed a matter of great delight and pride to see her perform on stage. Sadhana's son's accomplishment is another story in itself! A bright engineering professional, having a Master's and then a Doctorate from one of the most coveted universities in the world, he brings laurels to himself and the family. After 3 decades, now Sadhana looks back at the dream of her own career with remorse in mind but satisfaction in her heart!

She is determined to overcome her lost opportunities in career at her 60+ age now by rejuvenating her passion for creative writing, engaging in projects of social relevance and many more!

References:

1. Work Life Balance, key to employee performance in India (The Economic Times. 4 September 2020)

Chapter 8

Emerging Trends

No topic on emerging trends is complete without the profound and emotional discussion about the COVID-19 and its impact on us. While the pandemic has disturbed the natural sequences and trends to a great deal, this part of the book intends to look beyond! Some megatrends that are expected to govern our careers, jobs and even lives are worth discussing here. That would enable us to successfully ride over the big waves, before they engulf us. Also, of great interest would be to keep a closer eye on the new technologies that are round the corner.

Employment

When it comes to employment, during the pandemic most of the countries have reported negative growth in jobs. A report by European Union says, "Statistics and research results show that in recent decades, before the coronavirus pandemic, the EU's labour market witnessed an increase in female employment rates. Women's employment seems to have been more resilient than men's to the economic and financial crisis in 2008. This was due in part to long-term developments and changes in the institutional framework, but also to women's tendency to work in particular sectors and accept flexible working arrangements (such as part-time work or teleworking)."

The Report further says, "The coronavirus crisis, however, has had a harsher impact on women than on men when it comes to the labour market. One of the main reasons is that men tend more to work in sectors considered as essential economic activities (with the exception of healthcare), whereas women's work often involves contact with customers and clients, making teleworking impossible. Women have also been faced with increased childcare needs, reducing their ability to work, while enjoying a lower level of social protection owing to their working arrangements."

Similar trends are there in Indian sectors also. Despite all efforts, employment recovery appears to be insufficient to close the gaps. Workers whose labour market position was disadvantageous prior to the crisis (for example, women, young people, migrants, informal workers, and workers in lower-skilled occupations) have suffered disproportionately.

Future workplaces

Every lesson that the human race learns, it takes steps towards correction and prevention of previous errors or disasters (hopefully)! We have learnt that many, if not all, workplaces can be built to support hybrid working (partly physical and partly digital/virtual). It provided an opportunity for optimising resources, increasing efficiencies from the employer side as well as the employee perspective. Sustainability (by reducing transportation cost, workplace power consumption, time wastage) is a very important strategic advantage for corporates. For individuals, flexible working opportunities, better balancing of work and personal commitments and choice of work environment are very big assets.

Hygiene and personal habits have been re-ascertained. What remained so many years as an untalked of subject will now drive the way workplaces would be organised, keeping health and hygiene in mind. Another significant factor is the emotional or mental health of the workforce. There is a clear realisation that better emotional and mental health of workforce leads to better work output as well as satisfaction. Work-life balance is no more the individual's lookout. Workplaces would be designed to give a better balance between work and personal life.

Virtual communication has created entirely new mindsets. Their effectiveness, at least in the majority of the activities has enabled the world to shrink into the digital/virtual evens, enabling increased participation, global reach, more structured deliberations.

ILO Global Commission on the Future of Work stated: "Today's skills will not match the jobs of tomorrow, and newly acquired skills may quickly become obsolete." The ILO strongly recommended that governments, employers, and workers invest in lifelong learning. As well as narrowing the skills gap in your workplace, upskilling can lead to better recruitment and retention rates. In fact, skills shortages and lack of relevant experience are common causes of organisations' recruitment difficulties. Many businesses are remedying this by developing more talent in-house, including upskilling existing employees to fill hard-to-recruit-for positions and sponsoring relevant professional qualifications.

Global disconnect

Businesses depended so much on globalisation that the sudden disconnect shattered the fundamentals. The decoupling or disconnect of economies had already started earlier but the pandemic certainly endorsed how dependence on globalisation could create vulnerabilities. In the automotive sector, one has witnessed complete breakage of the supply chain from established manufacturing centres in Eastern Asia.

Some of the world's major powers, such as the UK, the United States, Brazil, Russia, India, and parts of the European Union, had already started to favour "economic nationalism". The dominance of some countries for manufacturing, supply of raw materials, energy sources, cheap labour, etc. has shaken up the globalisation fundamentals. To mitigate such risks, as these nations plan their future strategies, there might evolve 4-5 large regions. With such a multipolar world (America, European Union, Asia with China and possibly India with two apex positions than one) might give rise to distinct economies, security networks, cultures, and laws.

Some critical issues that these poles would have to handle (other than resource sharing) are data privacy, standards, trade agreements, and more. With globalisation, it is like trying to fit a square peg into a round hole. It is also true that every region has its own specific priorities, problems and focus areas.

Transition shock

Some of our biggest societal systems and modern industries such as education, transportation, energy, food, and healthcare are in the midst of massive changes. Measurable climate change has established that it is no more a myth. Bound by international conventions and national commitments, these sectors are drivers to take fast actions and redefine their businesses.

Livestock production is cited as being responsible for 14.5% of greenhouse-gas emissions, and this has generated great support for going vegan or vegetarian, as well as the food industry working to develop meat substitutes that is as convincing as the real thing to satisfy reticent carnivores.

Fig. 1 - World is looking at vegan food as a great choice (Image from Pixabay)

I was a part of an Indo-Sweden industry event held in Stockholm in 2019. The banquet arrangements for the Indian and Swedish participants were excellent and very special. The chef, a young smart man of Indian origin presented to the crowd all those exotic dishes and the most relished one that day was Jackfruit Biryani. Raw jackfruit was curated into a lamb equivalent taste!

In the automotive domain, the debate will continue about what is the fate of IC engines (Internal Combustion engines), but it is a ground reality that manufacturers are looking frantically for alternative mobility solutions and lawmakers are having stricter stance toward greenhouse gas emissions, energy consumption and other environment and sustainability goals.

From e-cars to autonomous vehicles, the transportation industry is in transition as well to develop the next generation transportation that is safe, reliable as well as sustainable. In the energy sector, decarbonisation of power is the major focus. Emissions reduction targets agreed to as part of the Paris Agreement on climate change are being deployed in major sectors.

Rethinking of business processes

The experience where teachers struggled to educate the next generation amid stay-at-home-orders and the workforce was challenged to keep businesses running remotely while juggling all that came with the "new normal", set us rethinking about the established practices. The healthcare industry faced the brunt of pandemic waves first and subsequently public wrath for the inadequacy of facilities. Retails, food outlets, hospitality, supply chains, logistics and many more services underwent transformations.

As our experience is digitised, workforces feel threatened by automation and do not feel valued or protected by either companies or the government, as was more common in the past. The shocks of our transitions are still reverberating and will continue as we shift to the next phase of our experience in all areas, including the economy, technology, healthcare, social development, and more.

The world has started taking "circular economy" much more seriously. Indiscriminate "use and throw" habits need to be curtailed. According to World Economic Forum, "A circular economy is an industrial system that is restorative or regenerative by intention and design. It replaces the end-of-life concept with restoration, shifts towards the use of renewable energy, climinates the use of toxic chemicals, which impair reuse and return to the biosphere, and aims for the elimination of waste through the superior design of materials, products, systems, and business models. "

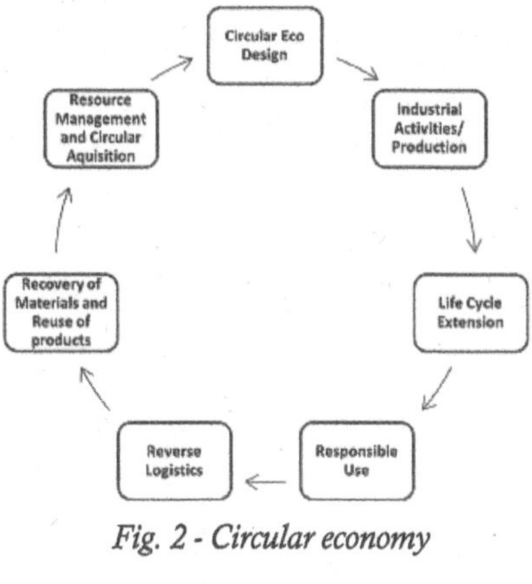

Fig. 2 - Circular economy

In fact, a circular economy is based on the idea that there is no such thing as waste. In order to achieve this, products are designed to last (good quality materials are used) and optimised for a cycle of disassembly and reuse that will make it easier to handle and transform or renew them.

Deep hybridity

Deep hybridity - a blend of the physical, biological, and digital worlds - is the future trend one should be aware of. Our new environment is likely to be a place where these worlds merge in our daily experience. Every organisation needs to consider how they offer physical and digital experiences that work seamlessly for those who interact with them.

For example, the Banking services (at least good private banks!) already have a multi-faceted approach to creating a frictionless experience and the right systems and infrastructure to support the personalised banking service, remote working, and online support for customers. Every organisation must now consider how they can provide products and services in the physical as well as the digital world.

Industry 4.0 (or Fourth Industrial Revolution) is all about cyber-physical systems and using technology to dramatically change our world. It may have begun in the manufacturing world where sensors and smart machines facilitated production, but it is now impacting nearly every industry, from healthcare to entertainment to energy and more. The opportunities are extraordinary in this next phase of our global economy.

Industry 4.0 has full potential for faster manufacturing procedures, better margins, lower costs, optimising processes, connected data, decisions made based on data and the list is endless! However, multiple legacy systems can hinder fast progress and bring in their own set of challenges. How companies truly maximise the power of Artificial Intelligence, Machine Learning, and data analytics - all combined with deep domain expertise will prove to be critical in the age of Industry 4.0.

Fig. 3 - Industry 4.0 (Illustration from Pixabay)

Industry 4.0 currently is focusing on the automation advancement of traditional manufacturing and industrial practices, using modern smart technologies. For the greenfield projects, it becomes relatively easy, cost-effective and efficient to adopt the principles right away. When an organisation with an existing legacy infrastructure makes a key decision to improve a process or line, lean improvements are often the first step. This is an important first step to ensure additional automation and digitisation of a recently improved process. Otherwise, automation and digitisation will only produce more outdated outcomes faster.

Power of Data is the basis of spinning business processes into digitalisation, analytics, automation, and machine learning. This generates great opportunities for data scientists, robotics experts, manufacturing experts having analytical minds and such. Women will find that Industry 4.0 is a fertile ground to create new careers.

Significant technology trends

Artificial Intelligence, or AI, has already demonstrated promising applications in previous decades. However, its deep influence on how we live, work and think is yet to be fully established. AI is already known for its superiority in image and speech recognition, navigation apps, smartphone personal assistants, ride-sharing apps and so much more. Predicting behaviours (customer and market predictions, vehicular safety systems), enabling the authorities to make better decisions (in hospitals, police administration, law and order and many more), enhancing personal experiences (spa, education and learning, entertainment, etc.) and a plethora of unexplored areas would open up.

The AI market is expected to grow immensely. With it spreading its wings across sectors, new jobs will be created in development, programming, testing, support, and maintenance, to name a few. On the other hand, AI also offers some of the highest salaries today.

Machine Learning, often considered the subset of AI, is also being deployed in all kinds of industries, creating a huge demand for skilled professionals. It is predicted that AI, machine learning, and automation will create 9% of new US jobs by 2025, jobs including robot monitoring professionals, data scientists, automation specialists, and content curators, making it another new technology trend!

Robotics and process automation

Robotics and process automation is aimed at automating business processes such as interpreting applications, processing transactions, dealing with data, and even replying to emails. RPA automates repetitive tasks that people used to do. Its applications in manufacturing processes, remote locations, underground mining, etc. are well established.

Automation has a direct impact on the loss of many jobs. However, not all processes are expected to be automated. In fact, they cannot be! It is reported by McKinsey in one study that not more than 5% of occupations can be totally automated. On the other hand, P&PA is expected to create many other but different jobs.

Virtual Reality and Augmented Reality

The next-generation technology trends include Virtual Reality (VR), Augmented Reality (AR), and Extended Reality (ER). VR immerses the user in an environment while AR enhances their environment. Although this technology trend has primarily been used for gaming thus far, it has also been used for training, in simulation software (in Naval ships, Armed Forces, spacecraft, etc.)

Soon we can expect these forms of technologies being further integrated into our lives. AR and VR have enormous potential in training, entertainment, education, marketing, and even rehabilitation after an injury. These technologies are expected to be used for training doctors to do surgery, offer museumgoers a deeper experience, enhance theme parks, or even enhance marketing.

The global AR and VR market is expected to grow and create more opportunities in the trending technology. It is a fact that getting started in VR doesn't require a lot of specialised knowledge but basic programming skills and a forward-thinking mindset would come as assets.

Internet of Things (IoT)

Another promising new technology trend is IoT. Many "things" are now being built with Wi-Fi connectivity; thus, they can be connected to the Internet, and each other. Hence, the term "Internet of Things" or IoT. The Internet of Things has already enabled devices, home appliances, cars and much more to be connected to and exchange data over the Internet.

As consumers, we are already using IoT quite effectively. We can lock our doors remotely, can track energy consumption, stay hooked to the medical monitoring devices and seek doctor's advice if needed, track our fitness and club it with the diet plans and many more. However, businesses also have much to gain now and certainly in the near future. The IoT can enable better safety, surveillance, efficiency, and decision-making for businesses. The big advantage is quick data collection, integration in the system and immediate analysis leading to controlled action. It can enable predictive maintenance, speed up medical care, improve customer service, and offer benefits that we have not even imagined yet.

In this decade, we are just at the beginning stages of this new technology trend and the forecasts suggest that by 2030, a huge penetration of these IoT devices will be in use around the world. There would be a massive web of interconnected devices spanning everything from smartphones to kitchen appliances and trains to clinical visits. The global spending on the Internet of Things (IoT) is forecast to reach 1.1 trillion US dollars in 2022. New technologies such as 5G are expected to drive market growth in the coming years.

5G (5th Generation technology for cellular networks)

5G is no doubt the next technology imperative in cellular network communication. 3G and 4G technologies have enabled us to browse the internet, use data-driven services, increased bandwidths for streaming on digital platforms and so much more. 5G services are expected to revolutionise our lives by enabling services that rely on advanced technologies like AR and VR, alongside cloud-based gaming services. It is expected to be used in factories, HD cameras that help improve safety and traffic management, smart grid control and smart retail too.

Fig. 4 - Heart of cellphone: 5G (Illustration from Pixabay)

Just about every telecom company is now working on creating 5G applications.

Cyber security might not seem like trending technology, given that it has been around for a while, but it is evolving just as other technologies are! Any valuable resource always comes with a threat of theft. Data, information, and knowledge being the most precious resource in years to come, the security threats are there to stay!

The malevolent hackers will continue to find ways to get through even the toughest security measures. It is also in part because new technology is being adapted to enhance security. As long as there are thieves in society, there would exist police and guards. Cybersecurity will remain a trending technology because it will constantly evolve to defend against those hackers.

References:

9 trends that will shape work in 2021 and beyond (14 January 2021 Harvard Business Review)

Briefing Note October 2020 (European Parliamentary Research Centre)

Chapter 9

Women Empowerment and Leadership

Empowerment

In the context of employees or individuals at their work, empowerment is often defined as the ways in which the organisations provide a certain degree of autonomy and control over their (employees') activities. Making important decisions, taking actions, and still operating within the defined boundaries is the crux of empowerment.

Understanding women empowerment

Keeping the above discussion in mind, let us see the empowerment of women at the workplace.

Fig. 1 - Empowering women (Illustration from Pixabay)

The status, employment and work performed by women in society are the indicators of a nation's overall progress. Without the participation of women in national activities, the social, economic, or political progress of a country will be stagnated. The fact is that most of the women's domestic role is combined with economic activities and utilisation of their skill and labour to earn the extra income for the family, which makes the difference between a reasonably decent survival and humiliating poverty. Women constitute half of the humanity, even contributing two-thirds of world's work hours. A woman earns only one-third of the total income and owns less than one-tenth of the world's resources. This shows that the economic status of women is pathetic, and this is more so in a country like India.

On this backdrop, women empowerment is a much-talked-about and debated subject, and rightfully so! The struggle of women to get their rightful position in the personal, social, and economic space is eternal. Generations after generations of social reformers have greatly contributed towards women empowerment. The horizon of empowerment is thankfully expanding and encompassing several aspects of women and their lives.

Empowering women and supporting gender equality are the stated aims of many development projects; this is an area of focus that is also expressed in the Sustainable Development Goals (SDGs) of the United Nations. Different understandings and definitions of 'empowerment' abound, and the contested nature of the concept makes it challenging both to define and to measure women empowerment. The added complexity is that different measurement approaches can themselves serve to strengthen or undermine empowerment. In the limited context of the discussion here, women empowerment is a way of defining, challenging, and overcoming the barriers in her life, through which she increases her ability to lead her life on her terms. According to some experts, women empowerment can be defined in 5 separate categories, namely, social, educational, political, economic, and psychological.

Defining the barriers involves some subjectivity. Women experience subordination on a daily basis, regardless of their class. Such subordination assumes various forms like discrimination, disregard, insult, exploitation, oppression and even violence. It takes place within families, in society and also at a place of work. Workplace barriers are the major points of discussion throughout the book.

Brief account of women empowerment in India

There is evidence that historically the position of women in Indian society has been gradually deteriorating. In Vedic times, women had glorious social status that was equal to men in social and political lives, civil administration, and other significant roles. In due course, women were denied inheritance rights, property rights, the right to education, the right to remarry, etc. The strong emergence of the Varna System further pushed women down in the social and economic hierarchy. Though women were respected in their families, their rights were severely curtailed. Females were considered fit only for rearing children, doing household work and remaining homebound. During the subsequent times like Gupta period, the status was further brought down. Practices like dowry were well established and became norms in the social outlook.

The major dip however happened during the Mughal invasion of the Indian continent. During this period, society felt the need to protect children and women from the invaders and it probably led to wrong practices such as child marriage, Sati, purdah and such. Women were more and more confined to homes where they were expected to be away from the evil forces in society.

It was subsequently during the British Raj that the doors of European ideas became open for Indians. Social reformers like Raja Ram Mohan Roy, Pandit Vidyasagar and later Mahatma Jyotiba Phule worked relentlessly for the upliftment of Indian women. Abolition of Sati, permitting widow remarriage were some of the landmark legal reforms. On the other side, women's education, societal participation, financial rights, etc were very effective factors that led to women empowerment. These efforts were further endorsed in Free India through the establishment of constitutional rights to women.

Diversity and inclusion enable empowerment

Diversity and inclusion are the steps towards establishing workplaces that enable individuals to participate with full heart and abilities. Not just gender but other distinguishing factors such as persons with physical/mental disabilities, ethnicities, economic and social differences must be kept in view for creating an empowered workforce.

Devanshi Joshi is a 27-year-old, warm hearted, talkative, and exuberant young working woman from Delhi. She worked initially for 6 years as a sales assistant at a private Store. She greeted the customers with her infectious smile and helped them in selecting products to suit their requirements. Details about hundreds of organic food and personal care products on the display and in the inventory were systematically stored in her brain! With her excellent performance and capabilities, she is currently employed by Big Bazaar as a full-time employee. This appears to be a normal task, till one learns that Devanshi is a differently-abled person and suffers from Down Syndrome.

She recently participated virtually at World Down Syndrome Day organised by the United Nations, Geneva and narrated her journey to independence. Very special journey of a very special person to inspire the world. But her parents, Anil and Rashmi, never treated her as a "special child". The eventful journey of the family establishes the fact that her inclusion in all activities of life enabled Devanshi to lead almost a normal life.

Anil and Rashmi ensured that Devanshi went to a regular co-ed school in Nagpur to complete her 8th Std education. Later she completed 12th Std from the open university. In addition to the basic education, she soon acquired special skills and hobbies like yoga, photography, high altitude trekking and dancing. Talkative and communicative that she is, 4 languages known by her (English, Marathi, Hindi and Gujarati) give her full freedom to express herself!

Anil Joshi is an IT professional and worked with IBM. He says, "Devanshi is the first employee with neuro diverse condition, not just in the Future Group (Big Bazaar), but in the retail sector across India. After positive experience with her, the Future Group introduced internship programme and recruited over 30 individuals with neuro diversity in regular employment. The significance is that understanding about the Legal Capacity of persons with intellectual disabilities was, and still is, a grey area. This is where Devanshi being an icon of Election Commission of India also becomes significant. Systems may need to be tweaked by providing reasonable accommodation in line with the principles of Affirmative Action, if inclusion has to happen meaningfully."

The international award-winning documentary *Raising the Bar* covers the journey of Devanshi and her family and some others from India and Australia. She has received a national award from the President of India as "Best Employee". She was honoured with many other awards like the prestigious Helen Keller Award.

More than anything else, she now works for spreading awareness for equal opportunity for persons with Down Syndrome and keeps inspiring many others. Election Commission 2019 included her in an awareness film about accessibility and inclusive elections. Her key message is, "I am glad that I have been able to show that we can achieve many things in life, if we decide. My dream is to see many more persons like me become independent and contribute to society. Together we can, and we will make it happen! Because we are Born to Belong."

Women empowerment schemes in India

Fig. 2 - Women empowerment schemes (Artist- Durga Tilak)

Indian society in general follows a strong patriarchal system and presumes male superiority. The Constitution of India not only grants equality to women but also empowers the state to adopt measures of positive discrimination in favour of women. Some of the significant steps towards this direction are:

- Beti Bachao Beti Padhao scheme : It commenced in the year 2015 and aims at providing education to girls and their welfare. Other highlights are the prevention of violations in the interest of girls. To celebrate the birth of a girl child is also a social change included in the scheme

- One Stop Centre scheme: (April 2015) Its aim is to set up One Stop Centres (OSC), to be funded under the Nirbhaya scheme. It is also expected to provide support and assistance to women affected by violence in private or public places, irrespective of their caste, class, religion, etc.
- Women Helpline scheme: (April 2015) To provide 24-hour emergency and non-emergency responses to women affected by violence including sexual offences in private, public places, workplaces, etc.
- Ujjwala: (Dec 2007) For the prevention of trafficking and providing support for rescue, rehabilitation, reintegration of women and child victims.
- Other specific schemes for education, skill development, micro-financing, welfare, health, and rehabilitation, etc

National Policy Intervention and directions

National Policy for Empowerment of Women (NPEW 2001) was adopted in the year 2001, which laid down a comprehensive policy for advancement, development, and empowerment of women. Many things have been achieved in the last 2 decades but much more is yet to be achieved. Significant strides in global technology and Information Technology have placed the Indian Economy on the global economy map. The changing landscape has a greater impact on individuals, especially women in many ways.

These changes have brought in fresh opportunities in women empowerment on one hand and created new and emerging challenges, which coupled with persistent economic and social problems cause great hindrance in women empowerment.

Several paradoxical trends related to women empowerment are being observed. The current status of women with respect to human development parameters, legal rights to live and freedom from violence, economic and social discrimination etc. shows that a lot remains to be done.

A new policy is therefore drafted by the Government of India, namely National Policy on Women Empowerment 2016. Some significant priority areas as identified by this draft policy are:

- Health, food security and nutrition
- Education
- Economy
- Governance and participation in decision making
- Violence against women
- Enabling environment
- Environment and climate change

NPWE 2016 guides several sectors to issue more detailed policy documents and action plans, which are sector-specific.

Women's participation in the economy is one of the major indicators of empowerment. Economic sectoral policies are as under:

1. **Poverty**

   Women constitute the major poverty-affected population. In all the poverty eradication schemes, there is a need to have a focus on women citizens and their differential status.

2. **Increasing visibility**

   Increasing participation of the women workforce, quality of work allocated to them and their contribution to GDP are the indicators of the extent to which women have been mainstreamed in economic growth.

   Gender wage gap exists largely in agriculture as well as non-agriculture sectors. Unless these gaps are filled through policy deployment of pay parity and formalisation of women labour, their contributions cannot be accurately quantified.

   Having a financial identity, such as credit sources, insurance, saving schemes, taxation benefits, etc. would be a major step towards increasing economic empowerment.

   Women undertake a bulk of unpaid services (childcare, cooking, water and resource collection, healthcare, etc.) and this unbalanced contribution undermines their contribution to the economic growth of society.

3. **Agriculture**

   With the increased participation of women in agriculture, their ownership and rights over resources will be an important consideration. Easy access to the advancements and modern techniques to women farmers would be an important step to improve their participation.

Women are traditionally known for the conservation of genetic diversity Seed banks (collection, and preservation) and these collectives are very critical for sustainable development.

4. **Industry, labour, and employment**

Decent work, a fair and just environment, equal wages, social security measures, occupational health and safety are some of the important steps towards bringing in women in the mainstream industrial growth. Facilitating the movement of women from informal to more formal way of employment would be essential. Skilling of women in the traditional, new, and emerging areas would be important in positioning women in formal as well as informal sectors.

Entrepreneurial development must ensure women's participation in all sectors. Revision of Labour Laws and Acts for better inclusivity is the need of the hour.

5. **Service sector**

Women's participation in the upcoming areas such as data and communications, informatics, infrastructure, healthcare, software designing, programming and financial services is increasing to a great extent. Specialised business services are also opening doors to welcome women, particularly in high paid jobs.

Conducive infrastructural facilities such as toilets, restrooms, childcare facilities, etc. are being mandated at the workplaces. Enabling women to have access to banking will also be an important step towards increased participation.

6. **Science and Technology**

Technological needs of women in rural as well as urban areas to increase employment, access to healthcare, education and communication would be significantly different than men. Opening up Science and Technology to women and significantly higher roles will ensure their voice to be integrated in technological development. Women normally have a greater flair for research and development in Science and Technology. The horizon needs to be widened to cover the unexplored areas for increased participation.

7. **Governance and decision making**

   To promote women participation in the legislature, executive, and judiciary at local, state and national levels, reservations are already in place. Women should empower themselves to come forward and participate more meaningfully and in depth.

   Women's participation in legislation and corporate boardrooms must be taken forward through appropriate skilling and coaching.

Women Leadership

Political

At the national level, while the 2019 Lok Sabha elections saw an increase in the representation of women, only 14% of the Members of Parliament (MPs) in India are women. In the recent cabinet reshuffle of the Modi Government, in July 2021, a total of 11 women have been assigned the charge of ministership. This is a step towards women empowerment through strong women leadership.

At the state level, women make up only 9% of the elected candidates of state legislative assemblies. Globally, India ranks 122 out of 153 countries when it comes to women's representation in Parliament, according to the World Economic Forum's Global Gender Gap Report 2020.

Women's representation in panchayats in India, on the other hand, is relatively better, thanks to the reservations brought in by the 73rd constitutional amendment that ensures one-third of leadership positions for women. However, this increased representation masks the barriers that women face in getting elected or while in office.

Corporate

India ranks third in the world for women working in senior management positions, according to the Women in Business 2021 report by global accounting firm Grant Thornton.

The percentage of women in senior management for India stood at 39%, against the global average of 31%, which signals the changing outlook of Indian businesses towards working women. The percentage of women leaders across key C-Suite positions in the country also emerged higher than the global average in the report.

Globally, businesses with at least one woman in the senior management role increased to 90%. In India, this stands at 98%. As much as 47% of mid-market businesses in India now have women chief executive officers (CEOs) compared with 26% globally.

STEM

There is a third important area: women in leadership positions in the Science and Technology space. While there is an impressive list of accomplished women scientists who have proven their distinction in areas ranging from space to aviation and healthcare to pharma, the fact remains that there is a need to scale up the efforts for women leading Science and Technology initiatives at the grassroots level. Add sentence after the word "level": CII has recently published a book "Indian Women in STEM" which proudly celebrates such success stories.

The international scenario is not much different. Annually to recognise intellectual achievements in various fields of knowledge, Nobel Prizes are given. During the long period 1901 to 2019, more than 900 distinguished individuals have been honoured with Nobel Prize. Out of these 900, only 53 were women, which works out to be less than 6%. In the categories of Physics, Chemistry, Physiology or Medicine, there are only 19 women Nobel laureates!

When it comes to worldwide STEM researcher, women hold the share of 30%.

Nari Shakti Puraskar

Ministry of Women and Child Development, Government of India, celebrates International Women's Day on 8th March to recognise the achievements of women for the nation and recognises their contributions to society. On this occasion, the government confers Nari Shakti Puraskars to individuals and institutions in recognition of their service towards the cause of women empowerment, especially vulnerable and marginalised women. These awards are also aimed at providing an opportunity to young Indians to understand the contributions of women in the building of society and nation.

These Puraskars are awarded for outstanding work, preferably in exceptional circumstances, to individuals, groups, institutions, NGOs, etc. in the areas of economic and social empowerment of women. The criteria include encouragement to women for participation in decision-making roles, skill development in traditional or non-traditional sectors, facilitation of basic amenities to rural women, promotion of women in the non-traditional sectors such as science and technology, sports, art, culture, concretely and significantly towards safety and security, health and wellness, education and skill development, life skills, respect, and dignity of women etc. Efforts by the state governments or Union Territories in improving Child Sex Ratio can also be recognised.

Rightfully so, the tagline of the awards is "Compassion, Ability and Courage"

Nari Shakti Puraskar 2019

On 8th March 2020, a total of 12 awards were conferred by Shri Ramnath Kovind, Hon'ble President of India on 15 women for their outstanding contributions towards women empowerment in various sectors. Their life journeys and commitment to work are very inspiring and motivating to all fellow countrymen.

Hon'ble President of India with Nari Shakti Awardees 2019

During the interaction with the awardees, Shri Narendra Modi, Hon'ble Prime Minister, expressed that all these ladies started off in a very humble way with their careers and long, successful journeys. Aspiring for the highest award on women empowerment was not their ambition but their lifelong commitment, dedication and humane service earned them the honours.

A brief introduction to these awardees would be very interesting and inspiring to the readers. All these outstanding and wonderful women come from diverse sectors, cultures, regions, age groups, skills, social strata and truly represent the diversity in India. The common thread in all these women is that they identified and defined their barriers to growth. In some cases, it came earlier in their lives while in several other cases, it came at a much-advanced age. Once they defined their barriers, the next stage was to develop the courage and capability to challenge the barriers. The next stage was to then overcome/cross their barriers. The awardees are thus an epitome of women empowerment in the country.

2019 Awardees

Arifa Jan

Arifa Jan from Kashmir has taken up the task to revive the once famed handicraft, Namda, the traditional embroidered rugs. Namda rugs have been made from 11th century and they are not woven but felted. Layers of wool fabrics are beaten together and then brightly embroidered. With her handicraft enterprise, "Incredible Kashmiri Crafts", Arifa has not only been able to revive customer interest in Kashmiri rugs but also revived the interest of local artisans. She has created 3 manufacturing facilities that employ 25 people and more than 100 women have been trained in this traditional craft. Her love for the craft and the zeal to take it ahead has inspired many people around her.

Arifa graduated in Craft Management and Entrepreneurial Leadership in year 2010. She then went to Kyrgyzstan to attend the Business Exposure Training, where she received a diploma certificate from the Central Asian Craft Support Association in year 2013. She has been sponsored by the United States Government for the prestigious International Visitors Leadership Program, also getting the US Citizenship Eligibility Certificate in 2014.

Arifa Jan with her Namda art

She is the recipient of several awards for her contribution towards the revival of the ancient craft of Kashmir. Apart from being conferred the Nari Shakti Award on 8th March 2020, Arifa became one of those "Magnificent 7" who was chosen to handle the Prime Minister's Social Media Account on the International Women's Day.

Bina Devi

Bina Devi is fondly known as "Mushroom Mahila" for popularising mushroom cultivation. She grew a small portion of mushroom under her bed, and she soon realised that there was a good opportunity for her to expand her skills. She became known for inspiring women to become businesswomen through mushroom farming. Bina Devi became the Sarpanch of Dhauri Panchayat in Bihar for a block of 5 years. She trained farmers for mushroom and organic farming, vermicompost production and organic insecticide preparation at home. She is also engaged in dairy and goat farming.

Bina Devi, the Mushroom Lady

She has trained women of 20 villages in Forbesganj block under Araria district. She has been instrumental in popularising mushroom production in 5 blocks and 105 villages in Munger district, impacting 1,500 women. She has trained 2,500 farmers in crop farming and supported the formulation of Self-Help Groups.

Bina Devi is also involved in spreading digital literacy and trained over 700 rural women on how to use mobile phones. Due to her concerted efforts, she has redefined the meaning of agriculture in her village. She is a recipient of several awards in Bihar for her outstanding contributions to upliftment of Women and Agriculture.

Chami Murmu

Chami, a resident of Bhursa Village of Jharkhand, is known as the 'Lady Tarzan' of Jharkhand for her determination to protect the forests, local wildlife and improve the livelihood of locals. She has been the founder and secretary of Sahayogi Mahila Bagraisai and she is presently a member of District Panchayat.

Way back in the year 1996, Murmu began to plant trees. Over the last 25 years, she was involved in planting 25 lakh trees with support from more than 3,000 women. These groups have planted trees over 780 hectares of government and non-government land and developed watersheds to enhance groundwater levels in the region. In achieving this, Chami and others had to fight against the mafia. She has been on a mission to protect local wildlife by saving diminishing forests due to unauthorised activities of the timber mafia and Naxalites.

Chami Murmu addressing the fellow ladies

In recognition of her efforts, earlier in 1996, she had also received Indira Priyadarshini Vriksha Mitra Award from the Government of India and several other awards in the field of environment and social service.

Kalavati Devi

Born in 1960, Kalavati Devi is the lady mason, a driving force behind reducing open defecation in the district of Kanpur. Due to a financial crisis, she was forced to work as a daily wage labourer and took up mason tools in her hand. She felt disgusted when she saw the conditions around the slums of Raja ka Purwa and resolved to build a community toilet. She, along with her husband, approached local corporations for funding. They offered her a fund of ₹2 lakh, provided she raised another 1 lakh by herself. She took up the challenge and did come up with a good sum. As a result, she transformed her own community by installing a 50-seat toilet and then moved on to other communities.

Kalavati Devi would move from door to door explaining the importance of toilets. She organised meetings in villages and spread awareness on the importance of hygiene and sanitation. While supervising and assisting the toilet construction work, she realised her true purpose in becoming a mason.

Kalavati Devi- Rani Mason

She is responsible for building more than 4,000 toilets in the villages in and around Kanpur. Her indomitable spirit did not shake despite being a single earner in the family after the untimely demise of her husband and son-in-law. Her unparalleled contribution has been recognised by Neurobion Forte.

Kaushiki Chakraborty

Kaushiki Chakraborty is an Indian Classical vocalist and renowned exponent of Khayal and Thumri of Patiala Gharana. She also has learnt South Indian Classical Music. From the tender age of 2, she started singing with her mother, who was also her first teacher. She occasionally toured nationally and internationally with her father. Prior to learning music from her father, renowned vocalist, Pt Ajoy Chakraborty, she received training from Shri Jnan Prakash Ghosh.

She completed her schooling and college education in Kolkata and holds a Master's degree in Philosophy.

In 2012, she set up SVA (Soul Voice Aspiration), a non-profit charitable trust with the primary objective to preserve and promote Indian music of all forms and to encourage young and upcoming talent.

Kaushiki Chakraborty, Indian Classical exponent

She hosts a weekly talk show with singers and artists for a popular Bengali entertainment channel.

Kaushiki has performed internationally in more than 5 countries and has contributed more than 90 songs for various albums. In 2015, she founded 'Sakhi', an all women classical band as a dedication to famous mythological and historical women of India.

Kaushiki is the recipient of many national and international awards and has performed at innumerable musical festivals and conferences. She has been conferred with "Ustad Bismillah Khan Yuva Puraskar" by Sangeet Natak Akademi in 2010.

Nilza Wangmo

Nilza Wangmo hails from Alchi, a remote place in Ladakh. Nilza was born in 1979 and lost her father before her birth. With support from her mother's family, she was brought up in a village called Stok, in the high mountains. She completed her schooling in a missionary school. She had to drop out of college due to financial constraints.

Nilza in her traditional Alchi Kitchen

Nilza was very fond of cooking since her childhood. In 2016, Nilza started a business called "Alchi Kitchen" using a small business loan. It was the first-ever eatery serving Ladakh's traditional cuisine including some exquisite and forgotten recipes. She and her mother developed a menu using local condiments and ingredients. Constantly encouraging young women to be financially independent, Alchi kitchen has employed young rural women. Nilza has personally trained these women to cook, serve and manage the restaurant.

Today Ladakhi cuisine is reaching the world due to her entrepreneurial efforts. Nilza has travelled and represented Ladakhi recipes in several reputed 5-star hotels. She is actively involved in charitable activities and is associated with People's Action Group for inclusion and rights to build a society that is free of prejudices and promotes girls' education.

Padala Bhudevi

Padala Bhudevi is from Savara tribal community living near Visakhapatnam in Andhra Pradesh. She was married at an age of 11 years and soon had 3 daughters. She was ill-treated and abused by her new family. Soon her husband abandoned Bhudevi and the daughters, and she decided to continue her struggle for life with the support of her father, who was running a charity called "Adivasi Vikas Trust". In the initial days, she worked as day labour.

Bhudevi is a role model for women farmers and rural women entrepreneurs. She has been working for the development of tribal women, widows, Podu lands through a community-based organisation - Chinnai Adhivasi Vikas Society (CAVS), which was established by her father in 1996. She is also the Director of Manyam Grains Pvt. Ltd. And Manyandeepika Farmers Producer Company Ltd. She has been involved in spreading awareness about mother and child health/nutrition with the support from the Integrated Tribal Development Agency (ITDA).

She has travelled across 62 villages in 3 Mandals to actively address problems faced by locals and along with her team, she has collected seeds that some farmer families have saved over the years. Thus 125 varieties of seeds have been distributed to farmers. Bhudevi also visited The Netherlands and China to get insights into seed preservation and cultivation.

Bhudevi, tribal activist

To ensure that tribal farmers get a better price for their produce and have access to nutritious food for their families, Bhudevi launched the Comprehensive Millets Resurgence Programme (CMRP) in 2016. She has established a millet processing unit with technical support from Krishi Vigyan Kendra which has generated livelihoods for about 60 tribal women and is supplying nutritious biscuits to about 15,000 residents and 47 hostels. She has been actively motivating women to participate in agro-entrepreneurial activities.

In recognition of her effort, she has been conferred with several awards at the state and national level.

Rashmi Urdhwareshe

Rashmi Urdhwareshe (nee Ranade) was born in Nagpur in a middle-class family which nurtured education and personal development. She was a bright and hardworking student and chose to join Engineering, which was an extremely male-dominated field. After passing out with a good degree in hand, she pursued Post Graduation after her marriage. After completing MTech in Electronics, she joined the Automotive Research Association of India (ARAI) as a Trainee Engineer and rose from the ranks to become the first Lady Director of the prestigious Automotive R&D and Homologation Institute in the year 2014.

While pursuing her career, she upgraded her skills and acquired various technical degrees and diplomas and developed expertise in Vehicle Testing and Certification, Ambient Air Quality, International standardisation, Quality Systems, alternative fuels, etc.

Rashmi Urdhwareshe: Automotive Technology expert

During her long career in the ARAI, Rashmi strived hard to develop technologies that would lead to safe, fuel-efficient and clean vehicles. She led by example how in otherwise male-dominated automotive domain, a woman can carve a leadership position for herself. She represented India at the various international forums in countries like the USA, Canada, Japan, UK, Switzerland, China, Korea, Germany, etc. and negotiated technical standards and regulations for vehicle testing. This enabled India to establish our own Safety and Emission regulations and carry out testing and approval of all vehicle models as per these standards. Rashmi also contributed immensely over 15 years at the international level at the United Nations Transport Sector on Vehicular Safety and Emission measurement and control.

Her contributions in bringing Electric Mobility solutions, green fuels (CNG, LPG, Hydrogen, methanol, etc.) on Indian roads are widely recognised by the Government of India as well as the Indian auto industry.

The leadership role that she played as Director, ARAI, has resulted in bringing the Institute at the global level in technology development on vehicle dynamics, light materials and manufacturing, Intelligent vehicle controls, electric storage systems and controls, engine development for efficient and clean performance and many more.

Rashmi has a strong mission of mentoring and training young professionals, especially women engineers, and takes up various projects at the national level towards fulfilling the mission. Women empowerment is a subject that is close to her heart.

Apart from a very illustrious professional career, she nurtures her hobbies such as gardening, extensive travel, instrumental music, and technical writing.

Rashmi has received various awards for her technical excellence, leadership, and women empowerment, including Distinguished Alumnus Awards, Businessperson of the Year, Industry Custodian of E-mobility Award, Rotary International Women Excellence Award, Lifetime Achievement Award, etc.

Sardarni Maan Kaur

Born in the year 1916, Sardarni Maan Kaur was an Indian track and field athlete. She holds world records in the Over 100 years old category for a variety of events.

Known as "Miracle from Chandigarh", Sardarni Maan Kaur started her athletic career at the age of 93! She stands as a testimony to the fact that it is never too late to begin anything that one wishes to do in life. Her son, Gurdev Singh, who is also an athlete, assisted his mother in her athletic pursuits.

She had won more than 20 medals in the Master's Games across the globe and was also associated with the Fit India movement. She was the oldest person to walk along the top of Auckland's Sky Tower. She had also won medals in javelin throw and shot-put. Recently, in year 2021, Man Kaur passed away.

Maan Kaur: Miracle from Chandigarh

Maan Kaur had a huge fan following due to her inspirational run in the world of athletics. Despite facing health ailments, she loved winning and had demonstrated that age is just a number.

Avani Chaturvedi, Bhawana Kanth and Mohana Singh

Avani, Bhawana and Mohana are the first women fighter pilots of India. For the trio, the sky has no limit. They were introduced into the IAF fighter squadron after the Government of India decided to open a fighter stream to women on an experimental basis. They were formally commissioned in 2016 to serve the nation by the then Defence Minister, Manohar Parrikar.

The flying fighters

Flight Lieutenant Avani Chaturvedi, born in 1993 is from Reva district, Madhya Pradesh. She obtained a BTech degree from Banasthali University, Rajasthan. Avani's elder brother, who is

an officer in the Indian Army inspired her to join the forces. She got selected for training at Hyderabad and became a fighter pilot in 2016. She was the first Indian woman pilot to take a solo flight in MiG-21.

Flying Officer Bhawana Kanth was born in Darbhanga, Bihar. Her father is an Electrical Engineer and her mother, a homemaker. As a child, Bhawana was fond of various sports. She received her BTech degree in Medical Electronics from BMS college, Bengaluru. Bhawana always dreamt of flying planes and she was selected in the Air Force Common Admission Test. She joined the fighter stream and received training at Hyderabad and became the first fully operational Indian Woman Fighter Pilot. She flies Hawk jet trainers. She has also done some modelling assignments.

Mohana Singh was born in 1992 in Agra, Uttar Pradesh in a family of soldiers. She completed her schooling in Delhi and BTech in E&TC from Amritsar, Punjab. Her father is serving the Indian Air Force and her mother is a teacher. While growing up, Mohana was fond of sports. In June 2019, she became the first woman fighter pilot of IAF on Hawk MK132 advance jet trainer. She has completed more than 380 hours of incident-free flying on Hawk Mk.132 and has experience of more than 570 hours of service flying.

Bhageerathi Amma and Katyayani Amma

By passing the Class IV literacy equivalent examinations, the beloved grandmothers of Kerala, Bhageerathi Amma and Katyayani Amma have proved that there is no age limit for learning.

Bhageerathi Amma was inspired to take the examinations conducted by the State Literacy Mission in Malayalam, Mathematics and Environment in the year 2019. At the age of 105, she is the oldest literacy equivalent learner under the Kerala State Literacy Mission. Her early quest for learning and knowledge ended abruptly when she was young and when she had to shoulder the responsibility of raising her younger siblings after the early death of her mother. Later, in her early 30s, she was a widowed single parent of 6 children. Nevertheless, she never let age get in the way of her pursuit of education. During her examinations, her 67-year-old daughter helped her out. Amma passed away in July 2021.

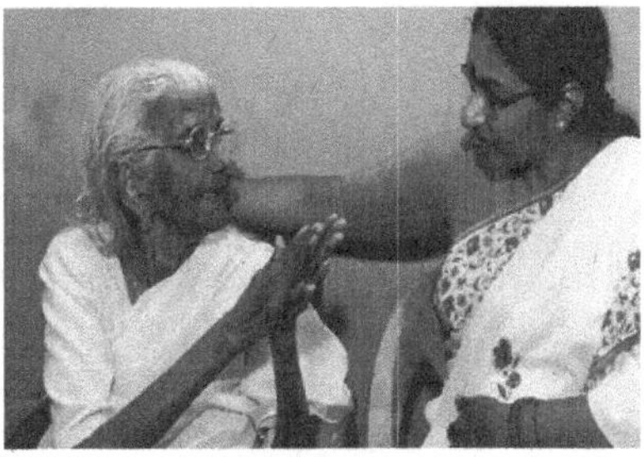

Katyayani Amma

Katyayani Amma was born in 1922 in a small town in Kerala. As a child, she was compelled to work and hence stopped attending school. She worked as a road sweeper and maidservant. She appeared for the literacy examination of the Kerala Government in 2018 and bagged the first rank, with a score of 98% marks.

She was given reading and writing lessons by her great-grand-children! She was 96 years old when she took up this uphill task and scored perfect 100 marks in English reading. She now aspires to clear the 10th Std examination when she turns 100! She also wants to acquire computer skills. She has been selected as the "Commonwealth Learning Goodwill Ambassador".

Tashi Malik and Nungshi Malik

Tashi and Nungshi Malik, born in 1991 are the first siblings to climb Seven Summits and reach the North and South Poles and complete the Adventures Grand Slam and Three Poles Challenge.

Due to their indomitable courage, at the age of 23, Tashi and Nungshi, the twin sisters became 6 Guinness World Record Holders. They are born to an Army officer. The girls completed their schooling from various schools in different states. In 2013, they completed a degree in Journalism and Mass Communication from Sikkim Manipal University. In 2015, they graduated in Sports and Exercise from New Zealand.

Hockey and athletics players Tashi and Nungshi began their mountaineering career in 2009 after doing a course at the Nehru Institute of Mountaineering (NIM) at Uttarkashi. Later, they also completed a course in skiing.

Tashi and Nungshi Malik

They became the first twins to conquer Mount Everest in 2013. They climbed Kilimanjaro (Africa) in 2015, mount Vinson (Antarctica) in 2014, Puncak Jaya (Australia) in 2014 and Mount Elbrus (Europe) in 2013. In 2019, the twins led team India "Khukri Warriors" in the world's toughest race, "Eco challenge Fiji" that pitched 66 teams from 30 countries.

They established Nungshi Tashi Foundation in 2015 to develop mountaineering as a sport and empower girls. To promote adventure tourism and sports, they have established an outdoor leadership school in Doon. They have been awarded the Tenzing Norgay National Adventure Award 2016 and Leif Erickson Young Explorers Award in 2016.

References:

Draft National Policy for Women 2016 (Ministry of women and Child Development, Government of India)

Devanshi Joshi's speech *https://youtu.be/1ieR8Rp7-14*

Web Portal of Ministry of Women and Child Development, Government of India

CII- TNTDPC Book "Indian Women in STEM"

About the Author

Rashmi Urdhwareshe retired in June 2020 as Director of ARAI (Automotive Research Association of India). ARAI is the prestigious autonomous R&D and Homologation Institute located in Pune. Starting her career as Trainee Engineer, Rashmi rose through the ranks to take the coveted position as Director of ARAI in year 2014. During her illustrious tenure as Director, the organisation scaled new heights in technology, business excellence and R&D. Creation of Centre of Excellence in E-Mobility, Homologation and Technology Centre and several key facilities were the landmark achievements.

Rashmi holds master's degree in E&TC and several other professional qualifications such as Diploma in Corporate Directorship, Six Sigma Black Belt, etc. Her 38 plus years of industrial experience and expertise establishes her as a national and international automotive technology expert. She has immense contributions in vehicular safety, air quality and exhaust measurements, Standards/Regulations, R&D and technology, E-mobility, alternate fuels and green technologies, quality systems and business excellence, and many more.

Rashmi has served as the Chair/Vice Chair of various national/ international bodies and contributed greatly to developing technologies and regulations on automotive safety, emissions, sustainable mobility, fuel efficiency and many more. She had been an integral part of Indian delegations and led the technical deliberations from the Indian side at UN-ECE WP.29 at Geneva for about 15 years.

She is currently President of SAE India (Society of Automobile Engineers). She is also Senior Advisor to Pune Knowledge Cluster

(PKC), which is set up under the directions of Principal Scientific Advisor, Government of India. Rashmi also provides Advisory and Mentorship service for Corporates, Educational/Research programs and Government agencies.

Rashmi is the co-author of the book, *Total Quality Management*. She is a recipient of several awards in the areas of women empowerment, corporate leadership, engineering excellence, E-mobility, business excellence, quality excellence and many more.

For her lifetime contributions towards development of Automotive Technology, she was honoured with the 'Nari Shakti Puraskar' at the hands of the Honourable President of India on 8th March 2020.